The Elizabethan
Prodigals

THE
ELIZABETHAN
PRODIGALS

Richard Helgerson

UNIVERSITY OF CALIFORNIA PRESS
Berkeley   Los Angeles   London

UNIVERSITY OF CALIFORNIA PRESS
BERKELEY AND LOS ANGELES, CALIFORNIA

UNIVERSITY OF CALIFORNIA PRESS, LTD.
LONDON, ENGLAND

ISBN: 0-520-03264-0

LIBRARY OF CONGRESS CATALOG CARD NUMBER: 76-14305

To Marie-Christine

Contents

Preface

Though the five authors who together constitute the principal subject of this book occupy a secure place in the literary history of England, few, if any, of their works can be said to have made their way into the artifice of eternity. This in itself might justify the kind of contextual approach I have taken to them. It may be, as Coleridge remarked, that "nothing can permanently please, which does not contain within itself the reason why it is so and not otherwise" (though I think the statement would be truer were "the" replaced by "a" or "some"), but the fact is that the works I am dealing with have not permanently pleased. To treat them as detached and timeless objects would be an absurdity; for, despite the enormous popularity that some of them once enjoyed, none has passed current since the early eighteenth century, and few survived the decade of their creation. They quite clearly do not contain within themselves any very obvious reason why they are so and not otherwise. If we are to appreciate them at all, it must be in terms appropriate to their original context.

I hope, however, that this excursion into the territory between sociology, biography, intellectual history, and literary analysis will do more than enhance our appreciation of Gascoigne, Lyly, Greene, Lodge, and Sidney. Their generation founded the modern literature of their country. When they were born England could boast of no poet since Chaucer of major standing; within a few years of their deaths English literature might have rivaled that of any nation, ancient or modern. What a study of these men reveals is the difficulty of that accomplishment. The pressures that they felt, pressures that found expression both in the stories they told and in the lives they led, were shared by many of their contemporaries, by such men as Raleigh, Greville, Marlowe, Nashe, or Spenser. And the often disillusioning experience they had as writers provided the starting point for their immediate successors, Marston, Hall,

Donne, and Jonson. Even Shakespeare, who somehow escaped the most debilitating of the burdens shared by these other Elizabethans, returned again and again to the literary patterns that my five authors first explored. Though in the chapters that follow I say little of these other figures, a reader interested in them should find here matter relevant to his concerns.

Whatever help or provocation this book may provide others, it has benefited from a good deal of both on its way to publication. In at least one or another of its various forms, it has been read and criticized, whole or in part, by Don Cameron Allen (who unhappily has not lived to see its completion), Russell Astley, Jackson Cope, Donald Guss, Richard Lanham, David McPherson, Laura O'Connell, Alan Stephens, Karl Stull, and particularly by Michael O'Connell, who has patiently borne every version of every chapter. Its appearance in print has been speeded by the kind intervention of William Frost. And in its final stages, it has profited both from the secretarial skills of Kay Hudson, Melanie Ito, and Deborah Lowry and from the editorial ministrations of Robert Y. Zachary. To all, my thanks.

R. H.

Santa Barbara
1976

1
Patterns of Prodigality

When I first read Elizabethan fiction, I was struck by the fact that story after story begins in the same way—with a scene of moral admonition. Both parts of *Euphues* start that way, and so do some half-dozen of Greene's longer fictions, and another half-dozen of Lodge's, and just about as many more by lesser fry of the Rich, Saker, and Melbancke sort. Even Sidney's *Arcadia* has its initial episode of good advice. But not only the beginnings resemble one another; the plots that follow from them are also remarkably similar. Invariably the young man (it is always a young man) to whom the admonition is addressed goes out and does exactly what he has been told not to do. And, just as invariably, he suffers for what he does. He repents, or is imprisoned, or, more commonly, both. The stories do not, however, all end alike. In some the young man remains repentant and disillusioned, while in others he returns from defeat to a happy denouement which rewards his disobedience. These endings correspond to the two poles of Elizabethan fiction and of much other Elizabethan literature as well, the didactic and the romantic. Where one circles back to confirm the initial admonition, the other opens to allow forms of experience prohibited or unimagined by the admonisher. Yet despite these profound generic differences, the books are clearly part of a single literary, and perhaps cultural, phenomenon. Whether they end by confirming precept or experience, they agree both in focusing attention on the conflict between the two and in identifying that conflict with another, with the struggle between the generations; for, if the central character is invariably a young man, his admonisher is almost as invariably an older one, a father or father surrogate.

How could one explain these various similarities? The extraordinary popularity of *Euphues* certainly had something to do with it. Lodge, Greene, and a good many others began writing as disciples of Lyly, and they naturally picked up his plot along with his style. But the influence of *Euphues* will not explain all. Sidney was no admirer of Lyly, and he may not even have known *The Anatomy of Wit* when he began his first *Arcadia*. Furthermore, the pattern of admonition and rebellion was adumbrated in a number of other works written too early to have felt the Euphuistic pull, in Gascoigne's *Glass of Government*, in Pettie's *Petite Palace*, or in Whetstone's *Rock of Regard*. As these last examples suggest, the pattern also occurs in genres well removed from extended prose fiction. And though it does center on Elizabethan fiction, it cannot be found everywhere in it. Gascoigne's *Master F.J.*, Nashe's *Unfortunate Traveler*, and the romance episodes of Chettle's *Piers Plainness* may have an affinity with the type, but the works of Munday, Deloney, or Forde have little or none. Only on a level of remote abstraction (as in Walter Davis's *Idea and Act in Elizabethan Fiction*)[1] could anything like our common paradigm be fastened on these other books, and on that level it could be attached to almost any work of any period in any genre. Clearly that paradigm neither supplied the structuring principle for all Elizabethan fiction, nor could it be explained solely in terms of such fiction. To study the one was thus not quite the same as to study the other.

The scholarship that has accumulated around these texts opened the way to another approach. Some seventy years ago John Dover Wilson discovered that *Euphues* derived its plot from certain Latin school plays based on the parable of the Prodigal Son, and since then the label "prodigal son story" has been fixed on many Elizabethan fictions.[2] This information led two ways, one iconographic, the other sociological. The first proved a dead end. Prior and parallel to its adoption by the schoolmaster dramatists and Elizabethan storytellers, the parable had lived vigorously in biblical commentary and homily, in church window and wall hanging, in sacred play and puppet show, but little of that got into the fiction. Greene based his *Mourning Garment* directly on the parable, and Whetstone and Harington explicitly mention the biblical prodigal; but even these rare allusions reflect an insular understanding of the story, quite removed from the interpretive and iconographic traditions that flourished elsewhere. Particularly conspicuous is the lack of any repeated attention to the merciful resolution: the joyful reception by the father of his erring son, the killing of the fatted calf, the bestowal of the best robe, and the placing of a ring on the prodigal's hand and shoes on his feet. All this, which gives substance to the main theme of the parable both in St. Luke and in subsequent pictorial and literary representations, is absent from most Elizabethan prodigal son stories, even from those which end happily. Not the parable of the Prodigal Son, with its benign vision of paternal forgiveness, but rather the paradigm of prodigal rebellion interested the Elizabethans. To the question of why that interest was so general and so intense, the pedagogic context in which they encountered the story did, however, seem to provide the beginning of an answer. In school the paradigm was urged on them as an image of what their own lives would be if they disregarded the narrowly conservative precepts of their fathers and teachers. They were admonished, just as their youthful protagonists are, and the form of that admonition was often a prodigal son story—but a prodigal son story that ended in punishment rather than in forgiveness. Perhaps that teaching took hold. Perhaps some of the young men who were schooled in this way did come to feel that the shape of that didactic paradigm had a particular relevance to their own lives, a possibility that seems more likely when we consider that among those things they were warned not to do was to waste time on the kind of profitless writing that earned them their celebrity. Surely something in their experience, something more compelling than a formal literary influence, more compelling even than the vogue of *Euphues,* is needed to explain their obsessive reiteration of the pattern of prodigality.

But mere analogy, particularly an analogy so lacking in specificity, hardly justifies this leap from art to life. The authors themselves did, however, insist that the two could not be kept apart. In the Epistle Dedicatory to *Euphues and his England* Lyly said that the first *Euphues* was a self-portrait; Greene broke off his *Groatsworth of Wit* to announce that he and his prodigal protagonist were one; Sidney scattered various clues hinting that Pyrocles and Musidorus bore a more than accidental resemblance to their maker; Gosson retold the story of prodigality as his own without even a veil of fiction; and a number of others—Gascoigne, Whetstone, Pettie, Saker, Lodge, and Harington—joined in suggesting that they too were prodigals and that their prodigality was mixed up with their writing. They had wasted their youthful time on the poetry and fiction of love just as their protagonists waste time on love itself. But the very ubiquity of such claims creates a doubt. Do they represent life or merely a convention of art? The artfulness is undeniable, and it inevitably provokes our skepticism. Like their contemporary Raleigh, these men were inveterate role-players. But Raleigh's roles, as Stephen Greenblatt has recently shown, had a persistent connection with the experiences of his life.[3] Through self-dramatization, Raleigh exploited and encountered, manipulated and acknowledged, knew and expressed himself and his situation. For him, role-playing was, as is art itself, a way of shaping a world to match his imagined sense of it, but it was also a way of fitting himself to the inevitable exigencies of the world. So with the Elizabethan prodigals. When, at the end of the letter prefatory to his *Petite Palace*, Pettie announces his recantation, labels his work the "fruits of my former folly," and says that he intends to join Alexius, the reformed protagonist of his last story, in a pilgrimage, we smile in disbelief and suppose that he smiles with us. But his book does show other marks of discomfort which testify to a pressure, whether psychological or social, that Pettie playfully accommodates by associating himself with Alexius. There was surely not much of Alexius in him or much of him in Alexius, but the pattern of folly and repentance exemplified by Alexius's story did contain enough truth for Pettie's career to confirm it. After the *Petite Palace*, he wrote no more of love. His next (and last) book was rather an earnest and serviceable translation. Thus Pettie accomplished in fact the role that he had acted in fiction.

Anyone who knows the poetry and prose fiction of the last three decades of the sixteenth century will recognize in Pettie's equation of literature with youthful folly a note common to an entire generation. Yet modern critics (with the notable exception of Russell Fraser)[4] have been disinclined to take seriously such denigrating judgments—and not only because of their playfulness of tone. The very magnitude of the Elizabethans' literary accomplishment prevents our believing that they could have been so unsure of themselves and the worthiness of their undertaking. Though we have learned to appreciate "the anxiety of influence," "the burden of the past" which weighs heavily on writers who must follow a Spenser, a Shakespeare, or a Milton,[5] we have achieved no comparable appreciation for the anxiety of those who work without such models, in an atmosphere of doubt as to whether literature can or should be made in their time or in their language. Had the doubts of the Elizabethans remained only the dressing of a dedication or a preface, our disbelief might, of course, be justified. But that is not the case. Those doubts entered into the very stuff of their literary experience, determining the way they read the poetry of the past, the way they shaped their own work, and even, as we are beginning to see, the way they understood their own lives. Unable to ignore the suspicion that poetry was morally harmful, and equally unwilling to forgo it, they had to prove again and again that it might be made beneficial. They were thus forced to argue that their work, rightly understood, warns against the very wantoness it portrays, but such arguments only involved them in a maze of self-contradiction, revealing their dilemma— the dilemma of their generation—without resolving it. Listen, for example, as George Whetstone talks about the "chiefest" consideration that moved him to publish his "vain, wanton, and worthless sonnets":

. . . in plucking off the vizard of self-conceit under which I some-times proudly masked with vain desires, other young gentlemen may reform their wanton lives in seeing the fond and fruitless success of my fantastical imaginations, which be no other than poems of honest love, and yet, for that the exercise we use in reading loving discourses seldom, in my conceit, acquiteth our pains with anything beneficial unto the commonweal or very profitable to ourselves, I thought the "Garden of Unthriftiness" the meetest title I could give them.[6]

This is less a defense than a confession. The poems are honest, yet wanton; beneficial, yet worthless. They are the product of "vain desires," yet are published in the hope that they may serve as a warning to other young men, though against what we are not sure since the love they treat of is perfectly chaste. But the last part of the sentence abandons even the pretense of didactic use. The collection is called the "Garden of Unthriftiness" with the implication that those who read it (like him who wrote it) will be wasting their time! But, like Pettie, Whetstone can still find some comfort in attaching himself and his work to the paradigm of prodigality. "Think," he urges us, "that my beginning with delight, running on in unthriftiness, resting in virtue, and ending with repentance is no other than the figure of the lusty younker's adventure."[7] The "lusty younker," the parable's prodigal son, offered the embattled author a defense against the charge of unthriftiness. If his work could be made to show the unhappy face of the archetype of unthrifty youth, then it could not be entirely profitless. And what Whetstone's book shows, his life confirmed: he did turn from poetry to "graver work."

The careers of Pettie and Whetstone remind us of others. Like them Googe, Turberville, Saker, Melbancke, and Warner each wrote a book of poems or an amorous fiction in his twenties and then either fell silent or produced some more useful work. As Timothy Kendall remarked in defense of his *Trifles . . . devised and written (for the most part) at sundry times in his young and tender age* (1577), "Grave men grave matters; sportful youth must sportful toys rehearse."[8] Here in a sentence is the idea of a literary career as it existed in England when Spenser and Raleigh, Lyly and Sidney came of age. A poet was a youth beguiled by the sportful fancy of love. And indeed what are Colin Clout, the Shepherd of the Ocean, Euphues, and Astrophel—the roles which the greater Elizabethans played and by which they were known—but youths in love? Moreover, the careers of these men show something of the usual pattern. Raleigh first wrote of love in verse and then of history in prose. Very few of his poems date from the last twenty years of his life. Likewise Sidney broke off his Arcadian epic of love in mid-sentence, turned to more worthy pursuits, and died condemning his looser lines to fiery oblivion, while Lyly, regretting that he had "played the fool so long," stopped writing altogether more than a decade before his relatively early death. Only Spenser never turned his tippet, though in the preface to his *Four Hymns* he did make some apology for the amorous fancies of his "greener times." But if he alone succeeded in resisting the anti-poetic pressures of his age, pressures that confined poetry to a few short years of youth, it was in part by fashioning for himself a role that both acknowledged those pressures and turned them to his own advantage. There was of course much more than this to Spenser's reinvention of the poetic career, but the point is that for there to be a Milton, a Dryden, or a Pope it did need reinventing. A career of any sort, particularly in an age as given to histrionic self-expression and self-affirmation as the Elizabethan, is like a theatrical part. If the player speaks more lines or other lines than are set down for him, even if they win him some brief applause, he will eventually be regarded and will perhaps eventually regard himself with contempt. And if the play contains another part which allows him to express his repentance, he may well claim it as his own. This, I suggest, is what happened to a number of Elizabethan writers—to so many, in fact, that the poet's part and the part of the repentant prodigal almost merged.

Thus though I began with a fictional pattern, I end with the pattern of a literary career as it existed in England for at least the first three decades of Elizabeth's reign. This book is about the two patterns and the relation between them in the experience of five writers: George Gascoigne, John Lyly, Robert Greene, Thomas Lodge, and Sir Philip Sidney. But it may be objected that I have already moved too easily from one pattern to the other, and this despite the increasing willingness of critics to allow a blurring of the line that a few decades ago sharply separated art from life. That there is a heightening, coloring, simplifying, and arranging, a creating of fact even as we articulate it, in our most ordinary nonliterary utterances, and an equally inevitable grounding on experiential reality in the most extravagant literary work is now generally admitted. Yet the claim that many Elizabethan prodigal son stories were meant to have an unusually close relation to the lives of their authors does nevertheless seem to require some special qualification, for it would be hard to find a less lifelike set of works.

With the exception of Lodge's *Alarm against Usurers* and Greene's cony-catching pamphlets, there is little in these books of what Ian Watt, discussing eighteenth-century fiction, called "realism of presentation." In the sixteenth century all the usual marks of such realism—individual names, particularly of time, space, and objective detail, and a straightforward, naturalistic style—are conspicuously lacking. As Watt remarked, "The stylistic tradition for fiction [prior to the emergence of Defoe and Richardson] was not primarily concerned with the corre- spondence of words to things, but rather with the extrinsic beauties which could be bestowed upon description and action by the use of rhetoric. Heliodorus's *Aethiopica* had established the tradition of linguistic ornateness in the Greek romances and the tradition had been continued in the Euphuism of John Lyly and Sidney."[9] We may balk at the inclusion of Lyly in the line of Heliodorus, and Sidney would certainly have been unhappy to hear himself called a Euphuist, but in a more general way Watt's point is well taken. Neither the characters, the situations, the settings, nor the language of Elizabethan fiction could be easily mistaken for anything found in real life, even the deliberately artificial life of sixteenth-century England. Consider, for ex- ample, the opening sentence of *The Anatomy of Wit:* "There dwelt in Athens a young gentleman of great patrimony and of so comely a personage that it was doubted whether he were more bound to Nature for the lineaments of his person or to Fortune for the increase of his possessions." Not the most naive reader would expect to meet this young gentleman on the streets of Athens. One would hardly know where to look. No particular street is ever specified, nor is any building, date, family name, or detail of appearance. The style by itself should be enough to discourage any such futuile search. Its jangling antithetical balance of "patrimony" and "personage," "Nature" and "Fortune," "lineaments of person" and "increase of pos- sessions," suggests that we have left the real world far behind to enter the artificially ordered realm of fiction.

Yet somehow the twentieth-century editors of *Euphues* have

gotten the idea that "Athens" refers to a place very much in the real world, for in a note at the bottom of the page they write, "*Athens:* Oxford University."[10] What evidence have they? Their note refers us to a later passage where the reformed Euphues, discussing the education of a model youth, whom he names Ephebus, breaks off to lament the decline of Athens. His terms make it clear that this Athens is not a city, but rather a university. But why should we think it Oxford? Because Euphues, in distinguishing *this* university from the universities of Padua, Paris, Wittenburg, Cambridge, *and Oxford*, says, "I can speak the less against them for that I was never in them." But Lyly, as a glance at the title page of the first edition would have shown, *was* in Oxford. Is Lyly then to be identified with Euphues? In this passage we assume he is. We could not otherwise identify Athens as Oxford. And I do not think the assumption hazardous. It was shared by Lyly's contemporaries, some of whom thought "that in the education of Ephebus, where mention is made of the universities, that Oxford was too much either defaced or defamed." Lyly tells us this himself in an epistle to his "very good friends, the gentlemen scholars of Oxford," which he appended to the second edition of *The Anatomy of Wit*. There he also says, "I can neither crave pardon, lest I should confess a fault, nor conceal my meaning, lest I should be thought a fool." And surely a contemporary who missed his meaning would himself have been something of a fool.

But even if we agree that in the passage on the universities Euphues speaks for Lyly and Athens represents Oxford, how do we know that those relations hold good throughout the book? The answer is that we don't. We do, however, know that Athens is always associated with learning ("the nurse of wisdom," Euphues calls it), and that its opposite, Naples, is a center of urban sophistication ("the nourisher of wantonness"), and so we naturally suppose that this story of a young Athenian in Naples relates in some way to the experiences of university men in London and at Court. The fact that Lyly was himself a recent graduate and that he was living in London certainly encourages that supposition. And when in *Euphues and his England* Lyly announces that *The Anatomy of Wit* was a self-portrait, the tie pulls still closer. Are we then to take it that everything that happened to Euphues also happened to Lyly, that the book is really an allegorical autobiography? I do not think so.[11] His intention was, I think, more playful. He wanted to provoke curiosity without quite satisfying it. We now condemn such teasing as beneath the dignity of art, just as the eighteenth century condemned the "false wit" that its aesthetic theories were too narrow to encompass. Yet works as commendable and as various as *The Adventures of Master F.J.*, *The Shepheardes Calender*, *Love's Labors Lost*, and *Astrophel and Stella* play with our curiosity in much the same way. Where critics have tried to keep artworks in one pile and historical documents in another, Renaissance writers liked to mix the piles, to hint that the ostensible work of fiction might conceal a reality too private or too controversial to be openly uttered. In part they hoped no doubt to titillate and amuse, but they had as well the more serious object of maintaining literature's claim on truth.[12] And though the truths that interested them were perhaps more often moral or aesthetic, the contingent truths of historical personality and event had their place as well.

In the case of *Euphues*, the mere possibility that the narrative may be almost true gives consistency to the image of himself which Lyly endeavors to project—and that endeavor, rather than any more directly autobiographical purpose, constitutes the book's vital relation to its historical context. As it happens, there does exist documentary evidence in the autobiography of Simon Forman, who was a contemporary of Lyly's at Magdalen College, that the story of *The Anatomy of Wit* was drawn from life.[13] But to the reader of Lyly's book, this evidence is useless. The context it supplies is clearly not *the* context of *Euphues*, for though Lyly's experience with "the mayor's daughter of Brackley" (if indeed he had any such experience) may have furnished some details of plot, details which could as easily have been found in literary tradition, it has no relevance to any but the most private and restricted meaning of the book. Neither the style nor the thematic structure of *Euphues* is rendered more intelligible by knowing that Lyly had an adventure similar to Euphues'. Both style and structure do make more sense, how-

ever, when we consider them in the context of Lyly's position as
a recent university graduate, eager to make his mark in the
world of courtly society. Here are the reasons why the book is so
and not otherwise. Without some reference to those reasons, it
can hardly seem other than a curious and incomprehensible
freak, as much a *lusus naturae* as Gulliver in Brobdingnag.
Neither a fully autonomous artwork nor a veiled account of true
events, *Euphues* is a rhetorical display of its author's attainment
through experience (whatever its exact configuration) of wisdom to match his native wit. But only by placing it first in one
context and then in another until we find one that fits can we
know this.

The argument of the present book is that in one way or
another the larger context which fits *Euphues* also fits the works
of many of his contemporaries; that they, like Lyly, were trying
to reconcile their humanistic education and their often rebellious
tastes and aspirations; and that, again like him, they found in
the figure of the repentant prodigal a role that would do just
that. These conclusions result from inferences about intention
and context like those I've been making in the last several pages,
inferences that by their very nature are open to question. But
such inferences, however risky, are an inevitable part of literary
interpretation; and here they are supported by a variety of
evidence. The evidence includes: (1) explicit authorial avowal
(Euphues is a self-portrait of Lyly), (2) contemporary opinion
(Athens = Oxford), (3) telltale difficulties in the text (Athens is
a university, not a city as one would expect), (4) literary convention (the Renaissance use of allegory), (5) specific biographical information (Lyly had been a student at Oxford and was
living in London), and (6) more general information about the
historical setting (Oxford in the 1570's was subject to a good
many attacks like Lyly's). This list runs in order of decreasing
reliability; with the first sort of evidence we can hardly go
wrong, but with the last two sorts we rarely go right, or at least
we cannot with them alone prove we have gone right. An
author who proclaims his likeness to one of his characters may
not, in fact, have been much like him; but it is sure that he
wanted to be *thought* like him—and that intention is really what

we are after. But in the absence of such avowal, even a great many specific points of resemblance between author and character will rarely be enough to prove that the likeness was intended. As Richard Levin has written in a recent attack on allegorizing critics, "It seems clear that, if we are limited to internal evidence, we must adopt Bacon's criterion: the character should show 'a conformity and connexion with the thing signified, so close and so evident, that one cannot help believing such a signification to have been designed.' "[14] Needless to say, this criterion can rarely be met, which is probably why, when an author wanted the association to be recognized, he said so. Fortunately for my argument, each of my five authors does say so in one way or another, as do at least as many more of their contemporaries. The problem is that their saying is itself often in need of interpretation. And that is where the other evidence comes in.

Some of this other evidence we have already noticed in the shape of those two patterns we began with, each of which was marked by an historical regularity of distribution. The first, the fictional pattern of admonition, rebellion, and (usually) repentance, we found concentrated in the last quarter of the sixteenth century. It occurs elsewhere of course (for example, in *'Tis Pity She's a Whore, Robinson Crusoe, Tom Jones,* and even *Pinocchio*), but what attracts our attention to the sixteenth century is the great number of examples crowded into such a few years. The second pattern is the biographical one—short literary careers often ending in repentance. It too is very common; it is, in fact, only a local variation of the familiar paradigm that Petrarch describes in his *Epistle to Posterity:* "Youth led me astray, young manhood corrupted me, but maturer age corrected me and taught me by experience the truth of what I had read long before: that youth and pleasure are vain. This is the lesson of that Author of all times and ages, who permits wretched mortals, puffed with vain wind, to stray for a time until, though late in life, they become mindful of their sins."[15] And for Petrarch, as for the Elizabethans, love and poetry were a part of youth and its vanity. But again what strikes us in the sixteenth century is the regularity of occurrence.

This regularity encourages us to look outside the particular works for a part at least of their meaning. When we come on a lone dancer, we assume that his movements have significance in themselves; but when we find a whole village dancing, we look rather for a larger, communal meaning. So with our Elizabethan patterns of prodigality, whose distribution reveals still further regularities, subordinate to those we have already noticed. Three stand out with particular clarity:

First, a social and generational regularity. The men who wrote these stories were children of the mid-century, born, with the exception of Gascoigne, between 1545 and 1560. Moreover, they were gentlemen, or at least called themselves gentlemen. And they were well-educated, having all attended either Oxford, Cambridge, or one of the Inns of Court. For whatever reason, writers born much later than the 1550's or lacking either the same level of formal education or the same pretention to gentility were less inclined to write stories of prodigality or to proclaim themselves prodigals.

Second, a "paradigmatic" regularity. Though many of these men wrote stories of both sorts, they identify themselves only with their repentant heroes, never with their successful ones: Lyly with Euphues, but not with Philautus; Greene with Roberto, but not with Dorastus; Lodge with the usurer's victim in the *Alarm*, but not with Rosader; others reveal, though in different ways, the same predilection for public confession, Gascoigne in *The Posies*, Whetstone in *The Rock of Regard*, Pettie in the *Petite Palace*, Saker in *Narbonus*, and Harington in the notes to his *Orlando Furioso*. As well as circling back to their own beginnings, the didactic tales thus return the author to his official self. The more open romances, in which he may have reveled for a while, present rather the image of a finally unattainable other, a self forbidden by the inner and outer censor. This may surprise those used to thinking of the Elizabethan as an age of romantic Marlovian overreachers, openly rebellious against authority.[16] Their lives and their works do show plentiful signs of rebellion, but when it came to declaring themselves publicly, they invariably chose the guise of repentance. In some instances the repentance was no doubt less than halfhearted, and in others there had probably been little to repent (like Justice Shallow, prating "of the wildness of his youth, . . . and every third word a lie"). But whatever the facts may have been, they did apparently feel compelled to claim as their own both the wildness and the guilt.

Third, a chronological regularity. The literary production of these gentlemen-prodigals falls into three overlapping periods of about a decade each.[17] First come the heavily rhetorical admonitory works, then the romances of successful love, and finally the works of disillusionment: repentance pamphlets, satires, and "dark" romances. The first period, which centers on *The Antomy of Wit*, begins with Gascoigne's repentance in 1575, and includes along the way the literary retirement of a good many writers who never get beyond a first book or two: Whetstone, Pettie, Gosson, Melbancke, and Saker. Moral edification through experience, usually the author's own, is what they offer, and edification is what their titles promise: *The Glass of Government, The Rock of Regard, the School of Abuse, The Labyrinth of Liberty,* and *The Alarm against Usurers.* The sequel to *The Anatomy of Wit* initiates the period of (to overstate things slightly) romantic rebellion, and the pastoral romances of Lodge and Greene are its typical products. These are the years of the University Wits, of Lyly's court comedies, and the plays of Greene, Peele, and the early Marlowe. They are marked by less edification, less guilt, less autobiography, and a good deal less of the prodigal son story, which is invoked only to be overthrown in stories like *Euphues and his England, Pandosto,* or *Rosalind,* and is simply ignored in a good many others. But about 1590 the pattern forcefully reasserts itself. Greene leads the way with his *Mourning Garment,* his *Farewell to Folly,* his *Groatsworth of Wit,* and his *Repentance,* but something of the same spirit, though without its autobiographical emphasis, marks Lodge's last fictions as well. For the writers who survived the first crash in the early eighties, this is the period of repentance. Sidney repents and dies in 1586; Greene in 1592; Lyly falls silent about the same time and a few years later he too regrets the folly of his literary career; and Lodge soon joins him. Now of course not every one of their works, much less every work by every member of their class and generation, fits this three-period scheme. But it does apply in at least a general way to the poems, plays, and stories of writers otherwise rather far removed from the tradition of Euphuistic fiction. Sidney's Old *Arcadia*, for example, has much in common with the works of moral admonition, while the revised version fits both thematically and chronologically into the period of romantic rebellion. Or, to take the works of two authors who wrote neither prose fiction nor works in other genres based on the pattern of prodigality, Marlowe's *Tamburlaine* and the first four books of *The Faerie Queene* belong in spirit with *Pandosto* and *Rosalind*, but *Docior Faustus* and *Faerie Queene*, V and VI, are more in keeping with the darker, less optimistic, works of the 1590's.

These historical patterns bring us back round again to our initial observations and to our initial questions. Why then? Why there? And what does it all mean? I cannot hope to account fully for each of these regularities. The last in particular poses very special problems, for it would require a detailed, year-by-year history of the political, economic, social, and religious life of these two and a half decades—history of a sort that I can hardly undertake here. I will, however, say something in later chapters about the chronological setting of individual works and the separate chronologies of the various careers; but I should be able to do a little better than that with the other regularities, with the social distribution and the inclination to public confession, with the pattern of the books and the pattern of the lives. These would seem to be the result not of rapidly changing conditions, of what Fernand Braudel calls historical waves of short duration, but of longer waves, lasting a generation, or a century, or the lifetime of a civilization.[18] And these I can try to describe. The place to look is where the waves make contact with the future writer: in his social, moral, and intellectual formation, in the family, at school, and in the larger society as it impinges on him. So it is here, with the education of the prodigal, that I wish to begin.

2
The Mirror of Duty

The formation of our prodigal authors began in their families, and it is there that we should begin our inquiry. We should quietly slip in and observe the elder Gascoigne, Lyly, Greene, Lodge, and Sidney instructing their sons. But this the fragmentary records of history will not allow us to do. Of Lyly's father, a minor ecclesiastical official and son of a renowned grammarian, we know little more than a name and a few odd facts, none of which serve to illuminate his relations with his son.[1] A bit more has survived concerning the fathers of Gascoigne and Lodge. Both were knights and men of substance, and both left conspicuous tracks in the legal records of the day, tracks which reveal something of their paternal behavior, for the poet-sons were both disinherited. The precise causes of their disinheritance have, however, faded into the penumbra of time.[2] Slightly more circumstantial are Greene's remarks about his upbringing. Twice in his *Repentance* he speaks of "the friendly persuasions of [his] parents," whom he characterizes as "well-known and esteemed amongst their neighbors . . . for their gravity and honest life."[3] But only in the case of Sidney can we fill out these "friendly persuasions."

In 1566 Sir Henry Sidney wrote a letter of admonition to his twelve-year-old son Philip, who was then in his seond year at Shrewsbury School. The initial words of its various commandments give some idea of their content:

> *Let your first action be the lifting up of your mind to Almighty God by hearty prayer . . .*
> *Apply your study to such hours as your discreet master doth assign you, earnestly . . .*
> *Be humble and obedient to your masters . . .*
> *Be courteous of gesture and affable to all men . . .*
> *Use moderate diet . . .*
> *Seldom drink wine . . .*

Use exercise of body . . .
Delight to be cleanly as well in all parts of your body as in your
garments . . .
Give yourself to be merry. . . . But let your mirth be ever void of all
scurrilous and biting words to any man . . .
Be you rather a hearer and bearer away of other men's talk than a
beginner and procurer of speech . . .
Let never oath be heard to come out of your mouth . . .
Be modest in each assembly . . .
Think upon every word that you will speak before you utter it . . .
Above all things tell no untruth . . .
Study and endeavor yourself to be virtuously occupied . . .[4]

One cannot help being struck by the impersonality of these
precepts. We take up the letter expecting to penetrate the inti-
macies of sixteenth-century family life and find that there is no
intimacy to be penetrated. No waywardness in Philip prompted
his father's letter. Sir Henry was motivated rather by occasion
("Since this is my first letter that ever I did write to you") and by
nature ("my natural care of you"). He does his duty as a father,
just as he expects Philip to do his as a son. Biographers have
made much of the touches of individuality—as when Sir Henry
remarks, "You degenerate from your father if you find not
yourself most able in wit and body to do anything when you are
most merry"—but we should recognize that these serve primarily to animate an ideal of a rationally ordered existence,
freed to a large extent from the vagaries of individual character.
With no incongruity its printer of 1591 could recommend Sir
Henry's letter as "most necessary for all young gentlemen to be
carried in memory."

Sir Henry imposed on his son an impersonal standard of
duty, all the more compelling for its impersonality. Though he
selected precepts suitable to Philip's age and situation, they came
from a common stock available to any Elizabethan—the same
common stock that supplied Lyly, Greene, and Lodge in their
fictions. Six of Sir Henry's fifteen admonitions recur in *The
Anatomy of Wit*, three in Greene's *Gwydonius*, four in his *Mourning Garment*, five in Lodge's *Euphues' Shadow*, and four in his

Margarite of America. Some have rather long pedigrees. In advising Philip to "think upon every word that you will speak before you utter it," Sir Henry adds the homely reminder that "nature hath ramparted up, as it were, the tongue with teeth, lips—yea, and hair without the lips, and all betokening reins and bridles for the loose use of that member." Two centuries earlier the Manciple's mother, in the only episode of parental admonition in the *Canterbury Tales,* used the same illustration.

> *My sone, God of his endelees goodnesse*
> *Walled a tonge with teeth and lippes eke,*
> *For man sholde hym avyse what he speeke.*
>
> > (IX, 321-324)

But, of course, the recommendation that one hold one's tongue goes back a good deal further than Chaucer. In the *Disticha de Moribus,* Cato advises,

> *Virtutem primam esse puta, compescere linguam:*
> *Proximus ille Deo, qui scit ratione tacere.*
>
> > (I, iii)

And Isocrates in his *Ad Demonicum* anticipates Sir Henry's advice to think before you speak. "When you purpose to declare any matter, first shape with yourself how to speak the same. For in many it chanceth that the tongue runneth before the wit."[5] A young Elizabethan heard a great deal about holding his tongue, and most of what he heard came from figures imbued with a quasi-paternal authority. Father Chaucer may have been mocking both the Manciple and the Manciple's mother (though the proximity of this passage to the Parson's attack on story-telling and to Chaucer's own retraction suggests an undercurrent of seriousness), but there is no mockery in Isocrates, Cato, or Sir Henry Sidney. Isocrates and Cato represent the authoritative culture of Greece and Rome, and within that culture they adopted the authoritative paternal mode. Each gives advice as from a grown man to a younger one, Cato addressing his son and Isocrates the son of a close friend. Furthermore, in the Renaissance they were, with Cicero's *De Officiis* (another book of duties sent by a father to his son), the most widely distributed sources of ancient wisdom. Cato's *De Moribus* was commonly the first Latin book a schoolboy encountered after completing "Lily's Grammar" (itself prefaced by a *De Moribus* written by John Lyly's grandfather), and Isocrates was a usual beginning Greek text.[6] Nor were their lessons forgotten when schooldays were past. Ten of Sir Henry's precepts have their counterpart in Cato and thirteen in Isocrates.

Modern readers, eager to find individuality wherever they can, have not always admitted the extent to which Renaissance fathers expressed a settled ideal of behavior in advising their sons. In introducing Sir Walter Raleigh's *Instructions to his Son,* Agnes M.C. Latham suggests, for example, that sixteenth and seventeenth-century books of paternal advice draw rather from experience than from literature. They are parts, she says, of a relatively unself-concious genre.[7] But we need go no further than the book Latham introduces to discover that the relation of experience to literature is more complex than this. The last of Raleigh's ten precepts reads in part: "Serve God, let him be the author of all thy actions; . . . please him with prayer lest if he frown he confound all thy fortunes and labors like drops of rain on the sandy ground."[8] Three years before the birth of Raleigh's son, thirteen years before he composed his *Instructions,* and forty-two years before they were published, Rabbi Belossi advised his son Philador in Greene's *Mourning Garment,* "First, my son, serve God; let him be the author of all thy actions; please him with prayer and penance, lest if he frown, he confound all thy fortunes, and thy labors be like the drops of rain in a sandy ground."[9] It would be wrong to accuse Raleigh of cribbing; he was merely taking over, endorsing, and passing on to his son the wisdom that other fathers, in life and in fiction, had passed on to theirs. Whether first or last, some similar exhortation to godliness, though not in quite the same words, appears in the *Ad Demonicum* and the *Disticha Catonis,* in Sir Henry's letter and the letter Lord Burghley wrote to his son Thomas, in *The Anatomy of Wit* and *A Margarite of America,* and in several of Gascoigne's poems of admonition. Experience and literature, the ancients and the moderns, spoke to the Elizabethan with one voice, a voice echoing that which had thundered on Sinai. For the first of the Ten Commandments also recalls the duty God's children owe their heavenly Father. The Decalogue thus joined the *Ad Demonicum* and the *Distichs* in providing a model for Elizabethan fathers, another preceptual and perceptual framework to help reveal the shape of experience. In dividing his counsel into ten chapters, Raleigh may have been consciously adopting that mode, as Burghley adopted it before him. "Because I will not confound thy memory," Burghley wrote his younger son, "I have reduced [these advertisements and rules] into ten pecepts and, next unto Moses' tables, if thou do imprint them in thy mind, then shalt [thou] reap the benefit and I the contentment"[10]—and both, we might add, could reap the satisfaction of seeing the world in a conventionally ordered way.

To our eyes Moses' tables may, however, seem quite unlike the tables of Burghley, Sir Henry Sidney, Isocrates, or Cato. The biblical Commandments are concerned with what we now call morals, the others with manners. The Elizabethans emphasize appearance rather than reality, form rather than substance, the expression on the face rather than the disposition of the mind. The best known Elizabethan admonition concludes, "To thine own self be true," but the truth that Polonius and his real life counterparts propose is social rather than individual. Not only are their precepts conventional but also they teach a cautiously conventional mode of behavior. They aim at a sincerity (to use a term that had then little of the meaning it has since acquired) that fits itself to the public garment which it is destined to wear, not one that nakedly displays its untrammeled thoughts and feelings. Such indecorous self-indulgence Sir Henry terms "pert boldness" and against it urges Philip to hold his tongue. Wisdom comes not from within but from without. "If you hear a wise sentence or an apt phrase," writes Sir Henry, exemplifying his precept by borrowing it from Isocrates, "commit it to your memory with respect of the circumstances when you shall speak it"—this to a son whose most celebrated utterance was to be, "Look in thy heart and write." The line from *Astrophel and Stella* may not be quite the manifesto of self-expression that it was once thought to be, yet it does reveal a tension between an ideal of the heart and the quite different ideal that we meet in letters of paternal admonition. The Elizabethan fathers were, of course, aware of the conflict between mind and heart; their central endeavor was to reinforce the one and guard against the other. But they perceived no conflict, nor even a significant distinction, between morals and manners, terms for which their beloved Latin conveniently provided only the single word *mores*. The absence of such a distinction was the governing premise of the ancient rhetorical tradition, which Isocrates helped to found, and in which the others were educated. "Ye shall surely find," wrote Roger Ascham in *The Schoolmaster*, that handbook of mid-century humanistic attitudes, "that when apt and good words began to be neglected . . . then also began ill deeds to spring."[11] And this being the case, a temperate manner, like clean Latinity, was regarded as of essential, not merely contingent, importance. Such temperance might, they clearly hope, serve as a defense against the destructive turbulence that had characterized the religious, economic, social, and political life of England for more than three decades.

The individual precepts in letters like Sir Henry's may have been thoroughly conventional, but the urgency with which they were promulgated was not. In their lifetime the Elizabethan fathers had been upset by four changes in the official state religion; they had experienced the greatest redistribution of wealth since the Norman Conquest; they saw education and manners revolutionized by Renaissance learning and Renaissance courtiership; and those among them who exercised authority under Elizabeth had already known one sudden political defeat at the death of Edward and lived with the fear that the death of Elizabeth would bring another. They insisted on the cautious, self-protective order of conventional manners because they had reason to feel the peril of disorder. Truancy that to men raised in a more secure age might have seemed relatively innocuous appeared dangerously threatening to them. And so they presented their counsels of worldly prudence with great conviction and even solemnity. Listen, for example, to the postscript wich Lady Mary Sidney affixed to her husband's letter:

Your noble, careful father hath taken pains with his own hand to give
you, in this his letter, so wise, so learned and most requisite precepts for
you to follow with a diligent and humble, thankful mind, as I will not
withdraw your eyes from beholding and reverent honoring the same—
no, not so long as to read any letter from me. And therefore, at this
time, I will write unto you no other letter than this; whereby I first
bless you, with my desire to God to plant in you his grace, and,
secondarily, warn you to have always before the eyes of your mind these
excellent counsels of my lord, your dear father, and that you fail not
continually, once in four or five days, to read them over.[12]

How was a son to escape the feeling that such advice was indeed a matter of grave and awesome moment? Particularly
when it came accompanied by a warning of the terrible consequences of disobedience. "Remember, my son," Sir Henry
writes, "the noble blood you are descended of by your mother's
side; and think that only by virtuous life and good action you
may be an ornament to that illustrious family. Otherwise,
through vice and sloth, you may be counted *labes generis*, one of
the greatest curses that can happen to man." In signing himself,
"Your loving father, so long as you live in the fear of God," Sir
Henry further intimates that any falling away from the straight
path of virtue will cost Philip his father's affection as well as the
respect of his family. The disinheriting of Gascoigne and Lodge
suggests that more than affection might be involved. Sidney
was not only a descendant of his mother's noble blood, he was
the heir apparent of her two noble brothers, the earls of
Leicester and Warwick. In an age of inherited property and
personal patronage, young men were particularly dependent on
the good will of their fathers and others who stood above them in
the hierarchy of rank, wealth, and authority. The advice and
expectations of such men naturally weighed heavily.

But Elizabethan fathers expected more of their sons than
virtue and wisdom. Those qualities, valuable as they were,
hardly merited praise if kept in seclusion. They were rather to be
used and tested in an active life of service to the state. This is
what Sir Henry has in mind when he alludes to "that profession
of life that you are born to live in" and prays that God will make

Philip "a good servant to your prince and country." The story of how in sixteenth-century England humanistic learning came to be equated with gentility, and how both learning and gentility were turned to the ends of government has been often told and need not be repeated here. Two familiar quotations will suffice to illustrate the change in attitude wrought by the importation of humanistic ideas and their adoption by the Tudor monarchs. First a nobleman cited by Richard Pace in 1517: "I swear by God's body I'd rather that my son should hang than study letters. For it becomes the sons of gentlemen to blow the horn nicely, to hunt skillfully, and elegantly to carry and train a hawk. But the study of letters should be left to the sons of rustics."[13] And second the gentlemen commissioners of the cathedral school at Canterbury in 1541: "It [is] meet for the ploughman's son to go to the plough and the artificer's son to apply the trade of his parent's vocation, and the gentlemen's children are meet to have the knowledge of government and rule in the common-wealth."[14] That this was not merely a change in attitude but also a change in practice is suggested by the frequent complaints that gentlemen's sons were driving poor men from the schools and universities and thus depriving them of any hope of pre-ferment—as was the intent of the Canterbury commissioners. Lawrence Stone has calculated that by the 1570's, when Lyly, Greene, and Lodge were undergraduates, gentry made up about half the population of Oxford and over 80 percent of that of the inns of court.[15] The extraordinary recourse of gentlemen's sons to the seats of learning in the middle years of the century had, however, an unforeseen result. It quickly saturated the offices of the state with men trained in good letters, leaving few openings for those who came behind.[16] So in order to support themselves in as gentlemanly a fashion as possible and to catch the attention of potential benefactors, they turned to writing. Thus their work was, as G. K. Hunter has remarked, "largely a product of frustration."[17] It does not, however, often express frustration, as will that of the next wave of university educated writers, the satirists of the 1590's. But it does express rebellion, defensiveness, and guilt—an acute consciousness that they were not doing what they had been brought up to do.

If the younger Elizabethans felt frustrated, it was because they had so thoroughly absorbed the notion that a humanistic education should lead to a position of public responsibility. "To what purpose should our thoughts be directed to various kinds of knowledge," Sidney wrote his continental guide and teacher, the Burgundian humanist Hubert Languet, "unless room be afforded for putting it into practice, so that public advantage may be the result?" But then he went on to add the bitter observation, "which in a corrupt age we cannot hope for."[18] That the bitterness was born of neglect, we can hardly doubt. Two years later he lamented that "the unnoble constitution of our time doth keep us from fit employments."[19] We hear the same complaint in Rich, Pettie, Lyly, Lodge, and a good many others, and those who do not complain nevertheless make the usual assumption that the proper end of learning is public service. Gascoigne, for example, at his death not only acknowledged that responsibility, but passed it on to his son:

> *Come, come, dear son, my blessing take in part,*
> *And therewithall I give thee this in charge:*
> *First serve God, then use thy wit and art,*
> *Thy father's debt of service to discharge,*
> *Which, forced by death, her Majesty he owes,*
> *Beyond deserts, who still rewards bestows.*[20]

And even the lowly Greene, who, unlike these other men, had no native claim to gentility, and who, again unlike them, never occupied any political or military position, nor, so far as one can tell, ever sought to do so, claims that his saddler father "had care to have me in my nonage brought up at school that I might grow to be . . . a profitable member of the commonwealth."[21] But whatever his family background, Greene would have had ample opportunity to absorb the humanistic ethos and to take on some of the trappings of gentility at the Norwich Grammar School, one of the two East Anglian schools most favored by gentlemen's sons,[22] and at St. John's College, Cambridge, the college of Cheke, Ascham, and Burghley. Learning may not have been the royal road to gentility and its obligations, but it was a widely recognized and much frequented bypath.[23]

Thomas Starkey's *Dialogue between Reginald Pole and Thomas Lupset* has, since its publication in the nineteenth century, become a regular stopping place in discussions of humanism and the *vita activa*. Written in 1535, when King Henry's "great matter" and the labors of Thomas Cromwell were remaking the English commonwealth, it represents Lupset's attempt to convince Pole, Henry's kinsman and the center of a circle of English humanists in Padua, to give ear to the needs of his country and abandon "the pleasure of letters and private studies."[24] "For little availeth virtue," Lupset is made to argue, "that is not published abroad to the profit of other."[25] But for the Elizabethans, Starkey's *Dialogue* suggests a broader choice and a greater possibility than in fact existed. The question of whether public service was the proper sphere of learning was, in the 1530's, still a matter of debate, as it had been twenty years earlier in More's *Utopia*, but by the 1570's the issue had been settled in favor of the active life. And, in the 1530's, a humanist might still hope, as Starkey evidently did, that his knowledge might "come to fruition with the prospect of an important part in the shaping of the policy, and perhaps even of the very structure, of the state."[26] Two decades into Elizabeth's reign such hope had all but evaporated. The great changes in the order of government and society had been accomplished; theirs was rather a time of conservative consolidation.

Another dialogue, Lodowick Bryskett's *Discourse of Civil Life*, better illustrates the attitudes of this later period. It begins with a gathering at Bryskett's cottage outside Dublin sometime in the early 1580's "of certain gentlemen": Dr. John Long, primate of Armagh; Sir Robert Dillon, chief justice of the common pleas; Master George Dormer, the Queen's solicitor; Captains Christopher Carleil, Thomas Norreiss, Warham St. Leger, and Nicholas Dantry; and Master Edmund Spenser, recently secretary to Lord Grey—all men occupying posts of public trust, and among them one famous poet. In the course of their conversation the question arises of why Bryskett, who had long and ably served as clerk of the Council of Munster, has suddenly given over his post. "We suppose," says Sir Robert Dillon, and his supposition is agreed to by everyone present, *that a man of your condition and qualities should rather seek to be employed and to advance himself in credit and reputation, than to hide his talent and withdraw himself from action in which the chief commendation of virtue doth consist. And to say truly what I think, a man of your sort, bred and trained, as it seemeth you have been, in learning and that hath thereto added the experience and knowledge which travel and observation of many things in foreign countries must breed in him that hath seen many places and the manners, orders, and policies of sundry nations, ought rather to seek to employ his ability and sufficiency in the service of his prince and country, than apply them to his peculiar benefit or contentment.*[27]

In response, Bryskett talks lamely of the attractions of contemplation, of how the duty of high office belongs primarily to the well-born, of the thankless toil required by his former place; yet it is clear that, though he has found little satisfaction in public service and has had little opportunity to turn his humanistic ideals into practical policy, he sees no alternative to Sir Robert's position. All his study even in his partial retirement has been bent on that "ethic part of moral philosophy," "by which a man learneth not only to know how to carry himself virtuously in his private actions, but also to guide and order his family, and, moreover, to become meet for the service of his prince and country, when occasion of employment may be offered unto him."[28] That is, he has been studying to do that which he has voluntarily ceased doing. This contradiction, pointed out by Master Dormer, is resolved only when Bryskett reveals that he has been translating Italian books of moral philosophy, work which, in Spenser's view, will "verify the principal part of all his apology . . . because thereby it will appear that he hath not withdrawn himself from service of the state to live idle or wholly private to himself, but hath spent some time in doing that which may greatly benefit others."[29] Writing with the intent of moving other men to virtuous action thus emerges as the only acceptable substitute for action itself. And, as Spenser makes clear, his own *Faerie Queene* is a work "tending to the same effect."[30]

Aided by the Italians, Bryskett hopes to find a method that

will allow him and other Englishmen, "without spending of so much time" as the direct study of Plato and Aristotle requires, to "speedily enter into the right course of virtuous life."[31] Time is a commodity. Bryskett, despite his apparent retirement, does not want to waste any of it. The program of study he proposes to himself is thus strictly practical. Sidney's letter to Edward Denny betrays the same concerns. "Resolve thus," he advises his friend, "that when so ever you may justly say to yourself you loose your time, you do indeed loose so much of your life, since of life, though the material description of it be the body and soul, the consideration and marking of it stands only in time."[32] And then he goes on to list books, point out their application, and suggest how many hours a day and how many weeks or months in all should be devoted to each. In this preoccupation with time and practicality, we find another reflection of their humanistic upbringing, one of particular importance to the prodigality portrayed in their literary works. They do on occasion treat of financial unthriftiness; the last item in Whetstone's *Rock of Regard* is a story of this sort, as is Lodge's *Alarm against Usurers*. But pecuniary imprudence is only a part, and not often an essential part, of their vision of prodigality. Whetstone gives the name "The Garden of Unthriftiness" to a section of his book that has nothing to do with money, to a collection of "wanton" sonnets. He is unthrifty in the pursuit of beauty and in the celebration of love; he wastes not money, but time, wit, and learning, goods that should be spent in some way "beneficial unto the commonweal" and "profitable to himself."[33]

This ideal of thrift, which recurs in the mercantile metaphors of Elizabethan love poetry, the audits and accounts which always prove the lover a bankrupt, the "expense of spirit in a waste of shame," is very much the product of an educational system so intent on using every hour and so convinced that it knew how to use the hours profitably. In his recent study of *The Renaissance Discovery of Time*, Ricardo J. Quinones has traced such attitudes from Petrarch, through the Italian educators of the fifteenth century, to the Gargantuan program recommended by Rabelais in the early sixteenth century.[34] A glance at the time tables printed in Leach's *Educational Charters and Documents* demonstrates their prevalence in England, with this difference: where Gargantua had time set aside for exercise, for digestion, cards, and music, for outdoor activity, and for games and merriment, the Tudor programs make no such specific allowance. On the contrary, the statute on play at Westminster (1560) reads, "The boys shall never play without leave of the Dean . . . and then only in the afternoon, and not oftener than once a week for any reason; and in a week in which a Saint's day falls, no leave to play shall be given."[35] Instead they ply their books from 6 A.M. to 8 P.M. with three hours off for dinner and another hour for supper—a ten-hour working day! Only slightly less austere was the program which Lord Burghley devised for his ward, the twelve-year-old Earl of Oxford.[36] It included seven hours of academic labor and half an hour of dancing. And Oxford, in training for life at court, had French along with his Latin. The grammar school boys got their Latin straight, or perhaps diluted with small portions of Greek and Hebrew. And for both Burghley and the Westminster schoolmasters use was the criterion, as it was for Languet when he discouraged Sidney's interest in astronomy, geometry, and Greek: "You must consider your condition in life, how soon you will have to tear yourself from your literary leisure, and therefore the short time which you still have should be devoted entirely to such things as are most essential."[37] The same utilitarian concern finds expression in the letter Burghley wrote John Harington, then a Cambridge undergraduate. The Lord Treasurer recommends Cicero for Latin, Livy and Caesar for Roman history ("exceeding fit for a gentleman to understand"), Aristotle and Plato for logic and philosophy, but warns against "dealing with over great variety of books, which young men delight in; and yet, in mine opinion, they breed but a scattering of mind."[38] Such scattering was, above all things, to be avoided in pursuing the objective that Burghley, Languet, and the English schoolmasters had in mind: the production, as Burghley says, of "a fit servant for the Queen and your country, for which you were born, and to which, next God, you are most bound."

Lord Burghley's role in the education of Lyly, Sidney, Harington, and their generation demands some further attention. In a patriarchal state, deriving its moral authority from its likeness to the family, Burghley, whom Peele addressed as *parens patriae*, was the archetypal father.[39] He was, moreover, the most active and powerful advocate of the ideals of mid-century English humanism. Born in 1520 and educated at St. John's College, he was the pupil and brother-in-law of Sir John Cheke and the patron of Roger Ascham, and their views were largely his. Even in the letter to Harington, he takes care to recommend the practice of double translation that Cheke taught and that Ascham described. Ascham's *Schoolmaster* was dedicated to Burghley and begins with a debate in his chamber, a debate in which the Queen's first secretary, as Burghley then was, takes a leading part. He took that leading part in the educational affairs of the nation as well. Joan Simon records instances of his intervention in the governance of some ten schools, and there are no doubt a great many more such instances that have been left unrecorded.[40] As master of the court wards, he maintained a household full of young noblemen which became a model of aristocratic education, as did the "Certain Precepts for the Well-Ordering of a Man's Life" which he directed to his son Robert and the advice on foreign travel which he prepared for Edward Earl of Rutland.[41] Moreover, he was from the first years of Elizabeth's reign chancellor of Cambridge University. There were, of course, other men in positions of authority who took an interest in education, men like Leicester, Nicholas Bacon, Thomas Smith, Walter Mildmay, Anthony Cooke, Francis Knollys, or Francis Walsingham. In no other period of English history has pedagogy been so directly the concern of government, but even in that age no man had greater or more lasting influence than Burghley. Already a leading member of the Privy Council in 1550, before most of our writers were born, he was still a privy counsellor nearly half a century later when they were all dead or silent.

But Burghley not only helped govern the institutions that shaped these writers, he was directly connected with many of them. He was a close personal friend of the fathers of Sidney and Harington, an official "friend" of Sir Thomas Lodge, and a neighbor of Whetstone, who dedicated poems to Burghley's wife and daughter, *The Rocke of Regard* to his eldest son, and *The Censure of Loyal Subject* to the Lord Treasure himself. Both Lyly and Sidney wrote to him when they were at Oxford, Lyly addressing him (hopefully perhaps) as "his much favoring patron." Lyly's most recent biographer has been disinclined to credit Burghley with the kind of influence on *Euphues* which earlier scholars had suggested; but he does say that "everywhere we look in Lyly's career we find a Cecil connection," and he goes on to admit to a suspicion "that Lyly's own relationship with the Cecils was the pivot of his career."[42] The Cecil connection in Sidney's life diminished as he grew older, but it too was once quite close. Burghley acted as Sidney's guardian when his father was absent in Ireland and nearly became his father-in-law. Yet despite these various connections, Burghley seems never to have rewarded the literary labors of these young men, unless it was he who arranged Lyly's position with the Earl of Oxford, Burghley's son-in-law and former ward.[43] He did secure government preferment for Gascoigne and Whetstone, but only after each had vociferously renounced amorous verse and turned to more edifying literary projects, like Whetstone's *Censure* or Gascoigne's *Drum of Doomsday*.[44]

Peele's begging letter and its accompanying poem, he filed, in the words of Peele's biographer, "with [letters] from cranks and crackpots, such as 'Hen. Carter, a crazy person, to Lord Burghley; for leave to arrest Mr. Richard Handforth, whom he bitterly rails against'; 'William Hobby [who] desires Lord Burghley's leave to drive the Devil and his dam from treasure hid in the castle of Skimfrith, Montgomery Shire, April 28, 1589'; and 'Austin Metcalf's mad incoherent jargon, addressed to the Queen and Lord Burghley, by way of petition.' "[45] Nor was Peele the only poet to earn Burghley's disregard, as this verse to Elizabeth suggests:

> *Madame,*
> *You bid your treasurer, on a time,*
> *To give me reason for my rime,*
> *But since that time and that season,*
> *He gave me neither rime nor reason.*[46]

Lodge and Spenser echo the theme, both complaining that Burghley, the prime conduit of royal favor, neglected soldiers and scholars—and by scholars they evidently meant writers like themselves, for Burghley was generous in his support of historians and grammarians.[47] In a dedicatory sonnet, prefixed to the first three books of *The Faerie Queene*, Spenser tried to anticipate and thus disarm Burghley's criticism,

> *Unfitly I these idle rimes present,*
> *The labor of lost time and wit unstayed,*

but to no avail, as the opening lines of the second installment reveal:

> *The rugged forhead that with grave foresight*
> *Welds kingdoms causes, and affaires of state,*
> *My looser rimes (I wote) doth sharply wite,*
> *For praising love, as I have done of late,*
> *And magnifying lovers deare debate;*
> *By which fraile youth is oft to follie led,*
> *Through false allurement of that pleasing baite,*
> *That better were in vertues discipled,*
> *Than with vaine poemes weeds to have their fancies fed.*

The terms Spenser employs, "idle rimes," "lost time," "wit unstayed," "frail youth," "false allurement," "vain poemes," suggest that all poetry, even the poetry of *The Faerie Queene*, which, like Bryskett's *Discourse of Civil Life*, was intended "to fashion a gentleman or noble person in virtuous and gentle discipline," might be expected to violate the patriarchal and humanistic values that Burghley represented.

But how representative were Burghley's antipathies? That poetry occupied an important, indeed a central, place in the humanistic curriculum can hardly be doubted. Another glance at those grammar school timetables suffices to prove it. Prominent among the standard texts are Homer, Virgil, Horace, and even Ovid and Terence. Still more conspicuous are the many hours, particularly in the upper forms, set aside for Latin verse making. If education and government were closely allied in the sixteenth century, so were education and poetry. The work of

Gascoigne and his immediate contemporaries, mid-Tudor poets like Googe, Kendall, Turberville, Proctor, or Edwards, shows with great clarity the imprint of classroom exercises. "The distinctive voice of the earlier Elizabethan poet is," as one recent critic has said, "that of the schoolmaster exhorting or reminding possibly wayward youths."[48] And though the voice of poetry changes considerably as the century progresses, one continues to hear now and again that distinctive schoolmasterly tone. But such verse was neither what the later Elizabethans wished to write, nor what Burghley wished to discourage, though even it would probably have incurred his reproof had it gotten out of place. Classroom versemaking aimed at furthering eloquence and strengthening morals, not at producing poets. Furthermore, it was generaly confined to the earlier stages of a humanistic education, from ages seven to fourteen in the curriculum proposed by Sir Thomas Elyot in *The Governor*, and from the upper forms of grammar school to the first year or two of the university in the curricula actually enforced in English schools and colleges. From there ("in which time childhood declineth and reason waxeth ripe"), the pupil was to pass on to what Elyot calls "more serious" studies: rhetoric, logic, history, and, most importantly, moral philosophy.[49] In the opinion of the Jesuit pedagogue, Martin Antonio Delrio, "not only poetry, but drama, history, oratory, and literature generally should be studied only by young boys, not by adults, whose sole concern with these things should be to edit texts for boys."[50] Not many Englishmen would have accepted Delrio's ban on history and oratory, but few would have disagreed that poetry's place was at school—or perhaps in milady's chamber. Even Sidney, when put to the question by his friend Denny, and that at a time when he was composing his *Defense of Poesy*, does not recommend a single poem. Instead he urges his friend to study history and moral philosophy, the very disciplines that had been held up to him six years earlier by Languet,[51] the disciplines that in the *Defense* he claims are surpassed in their didactic efficacy by poetry. Down from the advocate's podium, Sidney quietly abandons that claim, and repeats the truths that he was taught.

But even in its more restricted role as pedagogical tool and occasional ornament, poetry provoked opposition. Though declaring it false, Elyot testified to the "opinion that now reigneth of them that suppose that in the works of poets is contained nothing but bawdry (such is their foul word of reproach) and unprofitable leasing [lying]."[52] A generation later Ascham is less sure of its falsity. Where Elyot had found in Plautus and Terence "wisdom, advertisements, counsels, dissuasions from vice, and other profitable sentences," Ascham responds with a sharp "Here is base stuff for that scholar that should become hereafter . . . a civil gentleman in service of his prince and country."[53] But despite his doubts, Ascham, like the still more severe Lawrence Humphrey,[54] is forced by their pure Latinity to admit the Roman comedies (properly expurgated, to be sure) to his ideal curriculum. John Rainolds would deny even that bare allowance; and though he remained in the minority, he was not without influence.[55] His rhetorical style begot the Euphuism of his Oxford pupils, Grange, Pettie, Lyly, Gosson, and Lodge, and his anti-theatricalism fueled Gosson's attacks on the stage, attacks which in turn provoked the replies of Lodge and Sidney.[56] Behind Rainolds's objections and the doubts of men like Burghley, Ascham, or Humphrey stood a long tradition of antagonism between Christianity and pagan culture which constantly threatened to reassert itself and to destroy the unstable union of piety and good letters which Erasmus had championed. That antagonism recurs in the lives of Gascoigne, Greene, Lodge, and Sidney and in the fiction of Lyly, whose hero, renouncing scholarship for divinity, muses to himself, "Why, Euphues, art thou so addicted to the study of the heathen that thou hast forgotten thy God in heaven? . . . Farewell, therefore, the fine and filed phrase of Cicero, the pleasant Elegies of Ovid, the depth and profound knowledge of Aristotle; farewell rhetoric, farewell philosophy, farewell all learning which is not sprung from the bowels of the holy Bible."[57] Easy as it is to dismiss the artful protestations of a Euphues, his glib words do touch on a problem that could not be so easily dismissed. We hear it pondered even by a renowned wag like Sir John Harington, who, in the midst of the self-satisfaction that he naturally felt on completing his *Orlando*

Furioso, was overtaken by a similar doubt, the fear that he would share the eternal torments reserved for "dissolute poets and other loose writers which have left behind them lascivious, wanton, and carnal devices."[58] Harington does manage to construct an answer to this fear, as do Sidney, Lodge, and Spenser, all of whom, like Harington, wrote formal defenses of poetry.[59] Yet the fact that he should have felt compelled to do so provides an eloquent reminder of how uncertain the moral position of poetry then seemed.

One way that schoolmasters found of countering that uncertainty and avoiding the charge of negligence was to use plays of their own composition, modeled on Terence, but freed of his Roman "filth." They naturally favored biblical topics, and the one that most readily served their turn was the parable of the Prodigal Son. Some two dozen plays in six languages, eight of them in English, attest to the extraordinary popularity of the parable in the century prior to the literary emergence of Lyly, Sidney, and their contemporaries.[60] A few of these plays belong to earlier dramatic modes, to the medieval morality or to the *sacra rappresentazione;* but most were written by professors of the new learning, men like the Dutch schoolmasters Willem de Volder and Georgius Macropedius or their English counterparts Richard Wever and John Redford, and reflect ideas of art and life very like those we have encountered in letters of admonition, pedagogical treatises, school curricula, and the educational policies of mid-century statesmen. But to these ideas the plays gave a dramatic form that would serve as model to Gascoigne, Lyly, Greene, Lodge, and perhaps even to Sidney. For, like the fictions of the Elizabethans, the prodigal son plays invariably begin with a scene of moral instruction given by a father, schoolmaster, or other wise elder to the young protagonist, whose disobedience puts the advice to the test and whose fall confirms its truth. Thus they dramatize the familiar warning that prodigality, foreign travel, love—anything that carries one off the narrow path of rational virtue—leads necessarily to repentance; and in doing so they served as a vehicle for the conservative fears of men who had lived through the period of dangerously rapid change brought on by the Reformation, men to whom the world necessarily seemed beset with perilous temptations. These plays reverse the normal Terentian argument of comedy. In them society is not remade; it is reaffirmed. They grant victory not to the young men, but to the old. They portray the wisdom of the paternal generation as true wisdom, not as the comic self-interest of the still lusty *senex* which poses as wisdom in Plautus and Terence. And in many of them the merciful denouement of the biblical parable is wholly forgotten. The prodigality of a son who defies his father's counsel is ruinous, not momentarily, in the third act of a play that will surely end happily, but forever. In two of the continental plays, *Rebelles* and *Petriscus,* the young men are saved only to fall subject to the rod they had so long hoped to avoid. In the English *Misogonus,* the son, who began as sole heir to his father's wealth, ends as a younger brother begging a meager share from his rediscovered elder. In *The Disobedient Child* the son is sent back to the shrewish wife he took in opposition to his father's advice. In *Nice Wanton* and *The Glass of Government,* the prodigals do not survive. They are hanged, flogged to death, or die of the pox. And even in those plays which do allow a happy return, such as *Acolastus, Samarites, Lusty Juventus,* and *Wit and Science,* it is a return to conformity with the precepts that had earlier been disregarded.

Equally foreign to the spirit of Roman comedy is the misogynism that marks these moralities of wayward youth. By making Science a woman and marriage the goal of Wit, Redford violates this schoolmasterly antifeminism and associates his work rather with the conventions of romantic allegory. But otherwise, women appear in prodigal son plays only as vicious harlots, shrewish wives, or criminally indulgent mothers. Despite the remarkable contribution that some individual humanists made to the education of women, the humanistic tradition, and particularly the tradition of Latin education, was aggressively hostile to women and their influence.[61] Even the humanists' objection to poetry had a partially misogynous basis; they saw poetry as soft and effeminate, weakening boys and leading them to pursue lascivious pleasure rather than manly and courageous accomplishment. And certainly the self-assur-

ance with which Elizabethan fathers asserted their patriarchal
rights derived in part from the same depreciation of women.
The humble and self-effacing footnote which Lady Mary Sidney
added to Sir Henry's letter shows the virtuous woman in her
proper place, "in the skirts of [her] lord."

I suspect that the Protestant faith of the Northern humanists
contributed to their misogynism, for they were accustomed to
representing Papistry in much the same way as they represented women: either as Whore of Babylon or as Holy Mother
Church, coddling the faithful like young children, giving them
eye pleasing baubles in place of the paternal Word. But of course
there are medieval and humanistic precedents for Protestant
misogynism, as there are for most Protestant attitudes. Here, as
elsewhere, the Protestants hatched the egg that Erasmus laid.
Erasmus had remarked on "the mischief that accrues when
mothers are allowed to keep their children in their lap until they
are seven years of age: if they want playthings do they not see
that monkeys or toy-dogs would serve them just as well?"[62]
And a good while before Luther, he had been a critic of the cult
of the Virgin. It is perhaps only an accident, but if so it is a
striking one, that in the *Colloquies* Erasmus should have chosen
of all relics Mary's milk for special ridicule. The drying up of that
milk of divine maternity and the displacement of the merciful
female mediator in the Protestant North of Europe contributed
to the extraordinary currency of the unforgiving version of the
Prodigal Son story, as it did to the development of tragedy.[63]
Misogynism removed the possibility of an escape from the
consequences of rebellion through love or maternal charity, a
possibility that we do, however, find dramatized in the only
sixteenth-century Italian version of the parable, Giovammaria
Cecchi's *Figliuol Prodigo*. The schoolmasters substituted for a
romantic (even Terentian) world of love and grace a world of
moral law and punishment, and in doing so they expressed a
hostility to beauty, poetry, and forgiveness against which the
English romancers of the 1580's had to wage a constant and
particularly debilitating struggle—a struggle that could be
undertaken only at the cost of making oneself an interested
party. It is as though a lawyer had to rob in the course of de-

fending a robber and thus become his own client: for the grace
(beauty) the Elizabethans defend is the grace (mercy) they need
for having prodigally pursued grace (love). And the difficulty
was compounded by their own Protestantism and their humanistic upbringing.

A central tenet of that upbringing was the notion that duty
properly defines the self. "To thine own self be true," said
Polonius, but he meant, "Be true to my precepts." Likewise,
Languet, in warning Sidney to be true to himself, conceived of
an identity determined rather by one's calling than by tempera-
ment or native inclination.[64] Sidney confirms his acceptance of
this idea when he advises Denny that the keys to self-
knowledge are Scripture and moral philosophy, particularly
Tully's *Offices*, the book of duties that Cicero wrote for his son
and that Burghley always carried in his pocket. So in the
prodigal son plays, paternal admonition serves as a guide to the
ideal self. In *Acolastus*, probably the most popular and most
often imitated of them all,[65] Pelargus tells his son to "live
according to my moral principles, for they are such as lead to no
repentance," and concludes by giving him a "memorial" to use
as the "model on which you may pattern your behavior, your
life, your thought. Study it assiduously, reflect on it, make it the
star by which you steer. Let it be for you a kind of touchstone by
which you test yourself, so you may learn inwardly to know
yourself. For if in any way, either in thought or deed, you
should deviate from its lessons, you may be sure that you have
sinned."[66] And in *Wit and Science*, Reason tells Wit,

> *Then in remembrance of Reason, hold ye*
> *A glass of Reason, wherein behold ye*
> *Yourself to yourself.*[67]

Reason and Pelargus both insist on remembrance as the key to
self-knowledge. Remember your father and his precepts, and
remember who you are. The idea of the self is given *to* the young
men, and thus to be remembered, but it is not *of* them. When
they rely on themselves, they go wrong: Wit when he "stands in
his own conceit," Acolastus when he follows Philautus (self-
love). And in going wrong, they destroy their own identity.

When Wit finally remembers to look into the glass of Reason, he sees only the fool that he has become, "Decked, by God's bones, like a very ass." Like the lovers of Alcyna in *Orlando Furioso*, Wit has undergone a Circean metamorphosis. He has lost himself, frittered away his essential being. "To be or not to be," the question that another prodigal, whose father also urged remembrance, would consider at the end of the century, underlies these plays.[68] To be, they suggest, means to emulate your father and to obey his counsel. Not to be means to stand in your own conceit, to follow the bent of your own disposition. They clearly imply that, in life as in art, any *essential* achievement requires right imitation.

The threat of a Circean transformation, of a metamorphosis from the self decreed by duty, haunted the mid-century humanists. "Do not permit yourself to be transformed into another person," warned Languet, and Ascham called Italy "Circe's court."[69] Moralized versions of *The Odyssey, The Metamorphoses, The Golden Ass*, and the biblical story of Nebuchadnezzar enforced the lesson, as did the plays. For they too present an admonitory image of transformation, whether it be the reduction of the prodigal to rags and tatters, as in *Acolastus*, or the more literal metamorphosis of man into beast, as in *Wit and Science* or *The Cradle of Security*, a play (now lost) which made such an impression on one sixteenth-century spectator that, so he tells us, "when I came towards man's estate it was as fresh in my memory as if I had seen it newly acted," and some sixty years after the performance he could still describe it in vivid detail.[70] By such potent means the threat of spiritual metamorphosis was impressed on our writers as well—and they echo it in their works.

The hero of Sidney's *Arcadia* laments that he is "Transformed in show, but more transformed in mind";[71] Spenser in Book II of *The Faerie Queene* makes Acrasia and her Circean Bower of Bliss the chief enemies of temperance; Greene likens the courtesans in his *Mourning Garment* to Circe;[72] and Harington finds in Ariosto's portrayal of Rogero's enticement by Alcyna (a type of Circe and the source of Spenser's Acrasia) "the very picture of the Prodigal Son spoken of in the scripture, given over to all unthriftiness, all looseness of life and conversation."[73] The disregard of wholesome admonition, intemperance, and the loss of identity were thus inextricably linked in their minds. And when Harington recognizes himself in Rogero, we begin to understand how this linkage might be extended to include even their literary activity. "When I was entered a pretty way into the translation," Harington writes,

about the seventh book [the book that treats of Alcyna], coming to write that where Melissa in the person of Rogero's tutor comes and reproves Rogero in the 49th staff:

> *Was it for this, that I in youth thee fed*
> *With marrow? &c.*

And again:

> *Is this the means, or ready way you trow,*
> *That other worthy men have trod before,*
> *A Caesar or a Scipio to grow? &c.*

Straight I began to think that my tutor, a grave and learned man, and one of very austere life, might say to me in like sort, "Was it for this that I read Aristotle and Plato to you and instructed you so carefully both in Greek and Latin, to have you now become a translator of Italian toys?"[74]

With that instruction came, as we have seen, a sense of what they were to be and do. They were trained to become "worthy men," Caesars and Scipios, political and military leaders. They were to benefit the commonweal by becoming, as Lord Burghley told Harington, "a fit servant for your Queen and your country"—and that duty could not be accomplished by writing of love, certainly not if such writing became more than a very occasional pastime. To write more was to abandon one's true identity for what Whetstone calls a "vizard of self-conceit."[75]

If we are to understand what these authors mean by their identification of themselves as prodigals, we must first understand this idea of a self defined by duty. Nothing more sharply distinguishes us from the Elizabethans than our idea of being, and nothing makes the dilemma of the Elizabethan writer less accessible. Ideas of progress, originality, sincerity, and self-expression, the "discovery" of an inner self and the redefinition of nature, all stand between us. The feeling that the true "me" derives from a pattern outside the self may not be foreign to our age, but we nevertheless label the willing acceptance of such a borrowed identity an act of *mauvaise foi*, an abnegation of existential freedom. And though guilt does still accompany change, it is more likely to attach itself to stasis. We measure ourselves against our fathers not to emulate, but to surpass them. The whole complex of ideas that made God, Reason, and Father grounds of being and surrogates for one another has virtually disappeared. The "memorial" that Pelargus gives his son is elsewhere in the play called "the sacred book of laws" or the "bibliorum codex." Pelargus is God, and in *Wit and Science* the father (or rather father-in-law) is Reason. Now if on stage a father could so easily be made to represent divinity or rationality, it is because actual fathers and schoolmasters, ministers and magistrates, all those who occupied places of authority, were ideally presumed to participate in those qualities. No wonder then if a young man felt that in disobeying his father he was disobeying the governing powers of the universe and of his own being.

But obviously something has been left out of my account of the influences that shaped these men. Indeed most literary historians would say (and with good reason) that what I have left out is considerably more important than what I have put in. The Elizabethans did not, after all, read only collections of precepts and prodigal son plays, nor did they encounter only the opinions of men like Elyot, Ascham, Humphrey, or Rainolds. They "scattered" their minds, just as Burghley advised Harington *not* to do. They read Greek, medieval, Spanish, and Italian romance. They knew Petrarch and Ronsard, Ficino, Bembo, and Castiglione. They studied the real Terence and his Italian imitators as well as the so-called Christian Terence. Their political world included, in addition to Burghley, more romantic figures like Elizabeth, Leicester, or Sir Christopher Hatton, who, in the words of J. E. Neale, "had danced his way into favour."[76] *Carpe diem* figured alongside "serve God and the commonwealth" in their repertory of available responses to time and its pressures. And if they had no example more recent than Chaucer of a great English poetic career, they could (and did) refer to Homer, Virgil, or Ariosto. So obvious and significant are these other influences, which fill our books of literary history, that it has become usual to distinguish between the Elizabethan fathers and their sons by identifying one group with mid-century English humanism and the other with Italianate and romantic courtliness, opposing "the wisdom of a Burghley" to "the graces of a Sidney."[77] Nor, despite some very obvious differences between them, are the two traditions always and inevitably opposed. On the contrary, some of the best and most influential studies of the period have argued that one was a natural outgrowth of the other, that in the younger Elizabethans we find merely "a larger and richer humanism than in the men of St. John's,"[78] and that the apparent "conflict is perfectly capable of being rendered by the *non minus pius quam facetus* formula" which occurs in the earlier English humanism of Sir Thomas More.[79] Having been built on the contradictory union of Christian faith and pagan eloquence, the humanistic tradition was designed to accommodate just such difference. What I would suggest is that with an upbringing like the one these authors had, with expectations and an idea of the self like theirs, even an enlarging and enriching might be dangerous, and that when attacked not even a formula allowing for the graceful intermingling of piety and wit would protect them.

If both civic humanism and courtly romance were to figure in a single life or a single literary work, they could not often do so as parts of a coterminous union, but rather in some dialectic of opposites, in a structure like that of the prodigal son story, with its pattern of admonition, rebellion, and guilt. I see humanism and romance as opposed members of a single consciousness, as the superego and id of Elizabethan literature, competitors in a struggle to control and define the self. Humanism represented paternal expectation, and romance, rebellious desire. Humanism provided the governing design, the beginning and the anticipation of an end, for most Elizabethan fiction and for much Elizabethan poetry and drama as well; romance provided an impulse, a motive for action, which carried the youthful protagonist from that beginning to that end or, on occasion, to another made in the image of desire rather than of moral expectation. As in the human psyche, superego and id could occasionally be made to complement each other. This is evidently what Elyot hoped in proposing that a child's courage should first be "inflamed by the frequent reading of noble poets" and later "bridled with reason."[80] A similar hope forms the basis of Sidney's *Apology for Poetry* and Spenser's *Faerie Queene*. But the union of poetry and moral philosophy was always ready to disintegrate at the first touch of social or psychological strain, as I think it did when Sidney got around to defending love poetry in the *Apology*, though his easy jocularity hides the extent of the fissure. And no wonder if it did disintegrate. Poetry and philosophy, romance and humanism, occupied quite different sociological niches. We look in vain for Petrarch, Ariosto, Heliodorus, or *Amadis of Gaul* in the curricula of schools and colleges, but we do find there an abundant selection of precepts and practical philosophy. The highest officers of the realm proclaimed the attitudes of conservative, mid-century humanism for all to hear; but romance, however much it might try to disguise itself as another form of humanistic admonition, lurked in the corners, passing in manuscript from hand to hand, never venturing into print without an apology. Humanism belonged to the hierarchical relations of father and son, schoolmaster and pupil, elder and younger; romance to the egalitarian commerce of friend with friend— those lewd and flattering companions whom fathers and prodigal son plays continually warn against. Humanism inhabited the masculine and misogynistic world of school and state; romance "had rather be shut in a lady's casket than open in a scholar's study."[81] In every father the humanist was inclined to see an image of the Heavenly Father; in every young woman a potential Eve; in every young man an Adam. Vice in a father or virtue in a woman was a paradox in the display of which an author risked the censure of the right thinking. But romance could hardly be written without daring such paradox.

The self-disparagement, even the moral self-disparagement, of these authors was, we will be told, thoroughly conventional.

And so it was. Repentance poems are hardly less common than love poems. Everyone wrote them, the repentant and the unrepentant alike. But we should not let that fact conceal the more important one that conventions retain their vigor only so long as they express a sense of reality shared by the writer and his audience. And, in this case, the reality was that the center would not hold. The marriage of Wit and Science continually threatened to go on the rocks. If these writers adopt defensive attitudes, it is because they have something to be defensive about; if they condemn themselves, it is because they feel some condemnation is in order; and if they begin their fictions with scenes of antiromantic admonition, it is because such admonition seemed a fundamental part of their experience. To assume otherwise is to suppose a degree of artistic detachment which would have made their works as foreign to their contemporaries as they have proved to some of ours. They saw their better selves in a mirror of duty which paternal admonition, schoolmasterly instruction, and governmental propaganda held up to them. Compared to that official better self, the romance-writing other could seem only a prodigal fool, "decked, by God's bones, like a very ass."

3
Gascoigne

"I have misgoverned my youth; I confess it."[1] So proclaims George Gascoigne in the dedication of his *Steel Glass*, and the proclamation echoes through his work. With the single exception of Robert Greene, no Elizabethan writer talks so much about himself, and not even Greene presents a more various, detailed, and convincing self-portrait. We hear of Gascoigne's study of philosophy, of his departure from and return to Grey's Inn, of his adventures as courtier, poet, and soldier, of his hunting, farming, and foreign travel, and a great deal of what half pretends to be and half pretends not to be his experience in love. Little of this would cause anyone but the most severe critical purist the kind of problem which I dealt with in discussing *Euphues* in the first chapter. Who could doubt that the experiences described in the "Dulce Bellum Inexpertis," or "Gascoigne's Woodmanship," or "Gascoigne's Voyage into Holland," or "Sat Cito, Si Sat Bene" really happened, or that their having happened affects the meaning of the poems? The claim of these works depends almost as much on their factual truth as on their verbal dexterity. Prove them false and no poetic license will save Gascoigne from being called a liar.

With the experiences of love we are, however, on that less certain middle ground between fact and fiction. Though the love poems contain no dates, no names of people or places, none of those details that would permit the skeptical reader to check the story out, they do nevertheless regularly include some intimation of truth. They deliberately tantalize, withholding names, but making an elaborate mystery of the withholding. "These things are mystical and not to be understood but by the author himself," reads a marginal note in *The Posies*, and as we turn over the pages we find "another mystery" repeated again and again. Yet the mysterious meaning is never more than half veiled. For in both collections of Gascoigne's early work, a presenter, whether the fictional G. T. in the *Hundred Sundry*

Flowers (1573) or the author himself in *The Posies* (1575), rou-
tinely identifies the occasion of each poem, and in so doing
betrays the presumption that poems like these do inevitably
have occasions; that they are an integral part of the courtly
conversation that goes on between lover and mistress, friend
and friend, hopeful job seeker and potential patron; that they
are, to use the jargon of the philosophers of language, ordinary rather than fictive speech acts. The settings range from
brief headnotes introducing single poems (e.g., "He wrote unto
a Scottish dame whom he chose for mistress in the French court
as followeth") to extended narratives which present connected
sequences of poems. There are three of these more complex
settings: "The Adventures of Master F. J." (in the *Hundred
Sundry Flowers*), "The Fruit of Fetters" (in *The Posies*), and "Dan
Bartholomew of Bath" (in both collections), each with a single
narrator and a single central character about whom the narrator
tells and whose poems provide the *raison d'être* of the work.

But what relation have these narratives to any historical
reality that the reader might have been expected to perceive?
One clue is the sobriquet applied to the hero of "The Fruit of
Fetters": he is called the Green Knight, a name Gascoigne gave
himself in the undoubtedly autobiographical "Dulce Bellum
Inexpertis." But there are other similarities as well.

> *I say his lots and mine were not unlike:*
> *He spent his youth, as I did, out of frame,*
> *He came at last, like me, to trail the pike.*
> *He pined in prison pinched with privy pain,*
> *And I likewise in prison still remain.*

> (I, 377)

The "Author" speaks these lines in "The Fruit of Fetters," and
since everything he says of himself could, on the evidence of
"Dulce Bellum Inexpertis," also be said of Gascoigne, we make
the assumption, which most "naive" readers would have made
anyway and with much less fuss, that when the "Author"
speaks in the first person singular, he speaks for Gascoigne,
because he *is* Gascoigne. Like the Green Knight, Gascoigne
wasted his youth, became a soldier, was captured and impris-

oned. Nor does the series of revelatory coincidences stop here. Both the narrator of "The Fruit of Fetters" and the Green Knight have been deceived in love, the Green Knight by a woman named Ferenda. Now Ferenda is also the name of the woman who deceived Dan Bartholomew of Bath, and lest we miss the connection the Reporter, who narrates the story of Dan Bartholomew, refers us to "The Fruits of Fetters," informing us

> *That that same Knight which there his griefs begun*
> *Is Batt's own father's sister's brother's son.*
>
> *(I, 136)*

All these hints—and there are many more of the same sort—are perhaps insufficient to allow a simple equation of Gascoigne with his characters or a direct attribution of their experience to him. A biographer who did so would be skating on very thin ice. But it is clear that Gascoigne wanted his readers to credit him with amorous adventures like these, even while he reserved the right to deny such conjecture if it should prove embarrassing— as it did in the case of "Master F. J."

The problem with "Master F. J." was that the world took its claim on reality all too seriously. The *Hundred Sundry Flowers*, of which "F. J." was the most conspicuous part, provoked such a violent reaction that its author found himself "derided, suspected, accused, and condemned" of immorality and libel (II, 135). The tale was judged scurrilous and its scurrility was presumed true. To the first charge Gascoigne pleaded guilty, arguing in his defense only that various worthy motives, which he enumerates and discusses in some detail, prompted him to publish even such a seemingly wanton work. But the charge of libel he denies altogether, mocking the suppositions of his readers, berating those too ignorant to tell fact from fiction, claiming that of twenty people he had questioned no two identified the characters in the same way, and swearing solemnly "that there is no living creature touched or to be noted thereby" (I, 7). But having expended considerable ingenuity to excite such speculation, Gascoigne well knew that the accusation of libel could not be quashed by ridicule and heated protestation. So he rewrote the story. He eliminated the three introductory

letters with their elaborate explanation of how the poems came
to be printed, of how Master F. J. had shown them to his friend
G. T., of how G. T. had shared both the poems and F. J.'s story
with H. W., and of how H. W. had indiscreetly passed both
poems and story on to the Printer. He eliminated too the English
setting, the English names, and the constant hinting that the
story dealt with real English happenings. Instead he placed the
narrative in "the pleasant country of Lombardy," rechristened
the characters with Italian names, and credited the whole to the
(fictitious) Italian storyteller, Bartello, claiming for himself only
the modest title of translator.

But he accomplished a more profound transformation as well,
one that made the poems an adjunct to the story rather than the
other way about. "I do dwell overlong in the discourses of this
F. J.," protests G. T., "especially having taken in hand only to
copy out his verses."[2] Bartello makes no such apology, with the
result that, where G. T. seemed the indiscreet purveyor of fact,
Bartello appears rather an inventor of fiction. And, as such, he is
able to give his work a more explicit moral form. This is particularly evident in the concluding paragraph. Where G. T. had
simply broken off, "as one that had rather leave it imperfect
than make it too plain," and gone on to present the poems of
"other gentlemen,"[3] Bartello tells us that his Fernando Jeronimy
spent "the rest of his days on a dissolute kind of life," that the
faithful Lady Francischina died of grief, and that the Lady
Leonora "lived long in the continuance of her continual change."
He concludes, "Thus we see that where wicked lust doth bear
the name of love, it doth not only infect the light minded, but it
may also become confusion to others which are vowed to constancy." To which the translator adds, "And to that end I have
recited this fable which may serve as example to warn the
youthful reader from attempting the like worthless enterprise"
(I, 453).

The fictionalizing and moralizing that we observe in "Master
F. J." was repeated in Gascoigne's work generally as well as in
his projection of himself. Beginning with *The Posies* in 1575, the
individual episodes of his life, like the individual poems of
"Master F. J.," are gradually subsumed under an ever more

simple and comprehensive pattern. The earlier version of "F. J.," the "Dulce Bellum Inexpertis," and many of the autobiographical poems in the *Hundred Sundry Flowers* are, by contrast, remarkable for the amount of relatively unpatterned experience they admit. Gascoigne does describe his "Voyage into Holland" as

> *This trusty tale, the story of my youth,*
> *This chronicle which of myself I make,*
> *To show my Lord what helpless hap ensueth*
> *When heady youth will gad without a guide,*
> *And range untied in leas of liberty,*
>
> (I, 354-355)

but it is only by a considerable metaphorical extension that his chronicle can be made to render this lesson or any other. "Dulce Bellum Inexpertis" betrays a similar disjunction between precept and example, the long, moralistic introduction, with its satirical survey of the various orders of society and its attribution of responsibility for war to "haughty hearts," "greedy minds," and "misers," having little or nothing to do with the equally long, but intensely personal, account of Gascoigne's own experience of war. And "Gascoigne's Woodmanship" attempts no moral, contenting itself rather with an elaboration of the ruefully humorous observation that, as student, courtier, and soldier, he has always shot amiss. But when we turn to his later works, to *The Glass of Government* (1575), *The Steel Glass* (1576), *The Drum of Doomsday* (1576), or *A Delicate Diet for a Dainty-Mouthed Drunkard* (1576), those books that "make amends for the lost time which I misbestowed in writing so wantonly" (II, 453), we find experience shut off at its end by a repentance that necessarily defines all that had gone before as wilful folly. The difference is between an alert, critical, and sensitive observation of life, a testing of idea by experience, and an acceptance of an idea which judges experience profitless. In both segments of his career, he seeks to attract patronage and employment by his literary work; but where up to, and partially including, *The Posies* his claim rests primarily on his wealth of experience and the qualities of mind which he displays in the literary presentation of that experience, he later emphasizes rather his repentance. The recital of precept, much of it translated from the works of Church Fathers, takes the place of autobiographical poetry and proves his submission to the severest conventional wisdom.

In his experience the earlier Gascoigne comes close to finding a justification for the misgovernment of his youth. It has made him an Everyman. Even before it hardens into that paradigm of prodigality which requires repentance at its end, his life assumes an archetypal design reminiscent of those commonplace accounts of the ages of man, of which Jaques's in *As You Like It* is the most familiar. Anticipating Jaques's infant, schoolboy, lover, and soldier, Gascoigne presents himself as student, lover, courtier, and soldier. And his repentance evidently prepares for the next step,

> *the justice,*
> *In fair round belly with good capon lined,*
> *With eyes severe and beard of formal cut,*
> *Full of wise saws and modern instances.*

Because of this experience, Gascoigne can proudly say to men younger than he, "Make me your mirror" (I, 14). He has passed through all the stages of youth and knows the dangers and disappointments of each. Though the self he ultimately affirms is the one dictated by precept, he has arrived at that affirmation by way of experience. He has taken risks, explored the limits of behavior. He has thus discovered for his younger contemporaries the nature of their common condition. Though a defeated one, he is a hero, and, as such, deserves the role he takes for himself of cultural protagonist. Without his having tested them, what would his readers know of either law or mercy? By his success or failure, they govern their lives. Gascoigne thus vaunts his accomplishment of misfortune. On it rests his claim to preeminence. "If hereafter you see me recover mine estate," he tells the young gentlemen readers, "or reedify the decayed walls of my youth, then begin you sooner to build some foundation which may beautify your palace. If you see me sink in distresses, notwithstanding that you judge me quick of capacity, then learn you to maintain yourselves swimming in prosperity and eschew betimes the whirlpool of misgovernment" (I, 14). Nor was Gascoigne's sense of accomplishment misplaced. George Whetstone, in whose Stamford home he died and whose *Rock of Regard* imitates *The Posies*, was only the first to trim his sails to the antiromantic wind Gascoigne found blowing.

But, as I have suggested, had Gascoigne's contemporaries attended only to his last works, they would have been denied even the modest incitement to prodigality which we have gleaned from *A Hundred Sundry Flowers* and *The Posies*. No pride in experience, no sense that the wanton poetry of youth may serve the end of self-knowledge is allowed expression in *The Glass of Government*, *The Drum of Doomsday*, or *A Delicate Diet for Daintymouthed Drunkards*.[4] These works stay rather to the narrow path of *contemptus mundi* (Pope Innocent III's diatribe is translated in *The Drum of Doomsday*), a path that led Gascoigne to the worldly preferment that his earlier books had failed to procure.[5] In August of 1576, shortly after the publication of *A Delicate Diet*, he was employed by Burghley. The lesson seems to be that only those who vociferously disdain the world can share in its riches, while those who delight in beauty and romance lose even that small share of worldly goods which they may have had. This is clearly the moral of *The Glass of Government*, a work that draws so heavily on the pedagogical notions of the generation which fathered and educated the Elizabethan prodigals that it demands particular attention.

The scene of *The Glass of Government* is appropriately (considering Gascoigne's debt to the Dutch education drama) Antwerp. The fathers, like the fathers of so many Elizabethan writers, are rich burghers who have risen "by continual pains and travail . . . from mean estate unto dignity" (II, 9). Each has two sons, a quick witted elder and a more plodding junior. Though the fathers are aware of the gross impropriety of ambition, they think it "not amiss to bring up [their] children with such education as they may excell in knowledge of liberal sciences . . . then may they by learning aspire unto greater promotion and build greater matters upon a better foundation" (II, 9). With the subtle reasoning of one who would keep down his inferiors while continuing to rise himself, Phylocalus, one of the fathers, makes a careful distinction: "But if I be not deceived, all desire of promotion (by virtue) is godly and lawful, whereas ambition is commonly nestled in the breasts of the envious" (II, 9-10). Gascoigne admits, and in the end partially satisfies, this bourgeois "desire of promotion," yet the moral weight of his play is overwhelmingly on the side of order. Gnomaticus, the schoolmaster whom the fathers engage, bases the whole of his instruction on eight sentences which describe the obligation that a young man has toward each member of the fixed hier- archy of the universe: God, king, country, the ministers of God, the magistrates, parents, "thine elder," and "thy body" which is "the temple of God." Explained at length and reduced to tabular form by Gnomaticus, then turned into verse by the steady younger sons, Phylomusus and Philotimus, these prin- ciples occupy much the same place in the structure of this play as the Book of Laws, which Pelargus gives his son, does in *Acolastus*; they are the glass of government in which the young men are to find their own likeness and "learn," as Philocalus says, "what they are of themselves" (II, 13). Here again, an acquaintance with one's duty is the beginning and the end of self-knowledge.

Like all prodigal son plays, *The Glass of Government* is also a *speculum malorum*—a mirror of evil as well as of good. It features not only the two steady, if dull witted, sons, but two overly bright prodigals, Phylautus and Philosarchus, and a whole cast of low life characters who offer an implicit parody of the moral instruction of the good schoolmaster. In the first act the bawd, Pandarina, gives her niece Lamia a lesson hardly less senten- tious than that of Gnomaticus, whom we have just seen teaching his charges that man's first duty is to fear, trust, and love God. "I pray you," says Pandarina, "learn these three points of me to govern your steps by. First *Trust no man* how fair so ever he speak. Next *Reject no man* (that hath aught) how evil favored so ever he be. And lastly *Love no man* longer than he giveth, since liberal gifts are the glue of enduring love" (II, 25;

italics Gascoigne's). The two elder sons enroll in Lamia's school and think rather of versifying her heavenly beauty than Gnomaticus's "tedious traditions." Their fathers, learning of their debauch, decide to send them off with their juniors to the university. From there their fall is as amazingly rapid as the rise of their brothers. Phylautus is executed for robbery in Calvinist Heidelberg despite the favor of his brother who has become secretary to the Palsgrave, while Philosarchus is whipped for fornication in Geneva, the city of Calvin, where his younger brother is a minister. Whatever profit Gascoigne may have derived from his own wayward youth, he grants these prodigal poets none. They are allowed neither repentance nor self-knowledge. Looking into the glass of government, the reader should not find it hard to choose whether he wishes to resemble the dead Phylautus or his comfortably sinecured brother.

Within the tradition of the prodigal son play, *The Glass of Government* represents a change in perspective and a hardening of attitude which parallels the development of sixteenth-century humanism. By the 1570's, as we have remarked, the struggle to convince gentlemen of the importance of educating their sons in good letters had been successful. In consequence, Gascoigne makes prodigality result from nature rather than nurture. Phylautus and Philosarchus have received no more lenient treatment than their brothers. All have been schooled alike, first in "humanity," then in Gnomaticus's morality. The fault is not in the prodigals' environment but in themselves, in their quick though unretentive minds. Biblical commentary on the parable of the Prodigal Son offers some precedent for Gascoigne's innovation. Erasmus mentions "quickness of wit" (in the English of Nicholas Udall) as the particular gift of the younger son, while Cornelius à Lapide quotes Augustine to the same effect and cites a variety of other supporting authorities.[6] In none of these, however, does the Prodigal's intellectual gift cause his downfall. Nor is it likely that Gascoigne sought inspiration directly from the exegetes. In fact, nothing in his play, independent of our knowledge of his intermediate sources, would lead us back to the parable, much less to commentaries on it. Yet the similarity is not wholly fortuitous. Repentance naturally drew Gascoigne toward an interpretation of experience which echoes the familiar Christian mistrust of the creative mind. But, like the Dutch schoolmaster dramatists Macropedius and Stymmelius, and the anonymous English author of *Misogonus*, Gascoigne derived his interpretation not from biblical exegesis, but from secular pedagogical theory—and, in his case, specifically from *The Schoolmaster* of Roger Ascham.

Developing a point only touched on in his source, the *Institutio Oratoria* of Quintilian, Ascham defends at length a wit "hard, rough, and . . . somewhat staffish," preferring it to a quicker wit, "apt to take" but "unapt to keep."[7] The distinction had been made by the earlier humanist educators Peter Paul Vergerio and Juan Luis Vives, but in a significantly different manner. Vergerio's is the thoroughly empirical observation of an experienced schoolmaster who knows that different natures should be directed to different ends. He remarks, as Ascham will, that quick minds are likely to succeed in poetry, while slower ones will do better in "real studies and practical pursuits."[8] Vergerio avoids, however, Ascham's implication that a creative intelligence is of less value, or poetry an unworthy activity. Vives' comparison of the two sorts of intelligence is found not in his major treatise on education, the *De Tradendis Disciplinis*, though that does contain an extensive treatment of differences in natural inclination, but in his philosophical-psychological work, *De Anima et Vita*. Like Vergerio's, his discussion is based on observation, though supported by Galen's theory of humors.[9] He makes no value judgment. In comparison, Ascham's energetic pages seem an anatomy of wit, a satire on rapid learners.

Why should the gentle schoolmaster be so hard on quick wits? The most obvious reason is to balance the score. Parents and teachers tend to punish unjustly a slow but steady learner, while overpraising his quicker fellow. But simple rectification hardly explains the violence of Ascham's language or its scope. Behind his condemnation lies a fear that he shares with the more rigid disciplinarians we have encountered, a fear that the skeptical mind which tires quickly of conventional platitudes threatens the social order. The career he prophesies for the quick wit nearly resembles that of the less fortunate prodigals.

Commonly, men very quick of wit be also very light of conditions and thereby very ready of disposition to be carried overquickly by any light company to any riot and unthriftiness when they be young and therefore seldom either honest of life or rich in living when they be old. . . . In youth also they be ready scoffers, privy mockers, and over light and merry. In age, soon testy, very waspish, and always over-miserable. And yet few of them come to any great age by reason of their misordered life when they were young, but a great deal fewer of them come to show any great countenance or bear any great authority abroad in the world, but either live obscurely, men know not how, or die obscurely, men mark not when. (P. 22)

The prodigal mind is likely neither to attain or even to respect the private wealth and public position which, for Ascham, are the marks of success.

The two elder brothers in *The Glass of Government*, Philosarchus and Phylautus, might easily have been drawn after Ascham's description. Speaking to Gnomaticus, the servant Onaticus defines them as "quick spirited." The schoolmaster's response summarizes the moral of the action that is to follow. "Yea, but what is that to the purpose? The quickest wits prove not always best, for as they are ready to conceive, so do they quickly forget, and therewithal, the fineness of their capacity doth carry such oftentimes to delight in vanities" (II, 38). Their ready acquiescence to temptation shows them to be "light of conditions," their reception of Gnomaticus's lessons "ready scoffers" and "privy mockers," their end "over-miserable." The two younger brothers, Phylomusus and Philotimus, are also cut of Ascham's cloth. They strike six of the seven "plain notes" which Ascham abstracts from Plato to aid a teacher in recognizing "a good wit in a child for learning." They are "well endowed" (though not too well), "retentive," "predisposed to love learning," "willing to work," "glad to learn," and "eager to be praised." They lack only the suspect virtue that might lead to skepticism, "diligence to investigate": "He that is naturally bold to ask any question, desirous to search out any doubt" (pp. 27-31).

Gascoigne not only shares Ascham's estimate of quick wit; he rivals the schoolmaster's hostility to chivalric romance (both Lamia and Philosarchus have read deeply in *Amadis of Gaul*) and goes beyond him in questioning the moral effect of even classical literature. Here again Gascoigne moves in the direction of the more austere Church Fathers. St. Jerome, who himself repented having been more a Ciceronian than a Christian, interpreted the swines' food in the parable as "the song of the poets, profane philosophy, and the verbal pomp of the rhetoricians," an interpretation that was accepted by Augustine, Peter Chrysologus, and a number of other commentators.[10] Now for Ascham dining with swine had a quite different meaning. "Surely," he writes, "to follow rather the Goths in rhyming than the Greeks in true versifying were even to eat acorns with swine when we may freely eat wheat bread amongst men" (p. 145). The delicate balance of northern humanism, epitomized in the Christian Terence, depended on following the ancients in eloquence and the Goths in faith. Ascham had no more difficulty maintaining that balance than did the younger sons in *The Glass of Government*. But Gascoigne, who first overindulged in versifying and then over repented, shows how unstable the balance really was. Before coming under the tutelage of Gnomaticus, all four of his protagonists had been brought up in "humanity." They had studied Latin and Greek grammar and had read the *Colloquia* of Erasmus, Tully's *Offices* and *Epistles*, and certain comedies of Terence. For the slower witted brothers this was a harmless, and perhaps even useful program; for their elders, however, it was insufficiently furnished with specifically Christian morality. Gnomaticus comments that "although Tully in his book of duties doth teach sundry virtuous precepts, and out of Terence may also be gathered many moral instructions amongst the rest of his wanton discourses, yet the true Christian must direct his steps by the infallible rule of God's word" (II, 17). Now even Ascham said that, without the Bible, Plato, Aristotle, and Cicero "be but fine-edged tools in a fool's or madman's hand" (p. 116); but in the context of the play Gnomaticus's words take on an added insistence. Ascham writes as the champion of classical studies; Gascoigne's work is a Christian defiance thrown in the face of Terence. In the Prologue he writes,

> *A comedy I mean for to present,*
> *No Terence phrase; his time and mine are twain.*
> *The verse that pleased a Roman rash intent,*
> *Might well offend the godly preacher's vein.*

> (II, 6)

And in the play Virgil and Terence lead the elder brothers on their way down the road to dissipation.

For both Gascoigne and Ascham, whatever their differences of emphasis, the young mind, especially the quick young mind, must be carefully indoctrinated. It must be kept from any free, unguided experience of either books or the world. Gnomaticus suggests that perhaps the prodigals should be left to learn by experience only because all else has failed. "Give them leave a little to see the world and to follow any exercise that be not repugnant unto virtue, for unto some wits neither correction, nor friendly admonition, nor any other persuasion will serve, until their own rod have beaten them, and then they prove oftentimes (though late) men of excellent qualities" (II, 80). This worked for Gascoigne himself, but in *The Glass of Government* the prodigals' own rod is too harsh and they do not survive to prove themselves "men of excellent qualities." For his part, Ascham passionately opposed the notion that experience can take the place of supervised instruction. "Learning teacheth more in one year than experience in twenty, and learning teacheth safely, when experience maketh more miserable than wise" (p. 50). Ascham would deny all but the barest hope that prodigality might lead to self-knowledge. Only the choice between dull conformity and self-destructive delinquency remains. And Gascoigne, despite his own experience, seems to agree. Nowhere does the mid-century humanism that he and Ascham represent provide a model for a specifically literary career. And, since Chaucer, there had been no English poet great enough to furnish one. At best, poetry, if denounced and repented after the fact, might be excused as a folly of youth. And neither Ascham nor Gascoigne considered even that meager best a likely possibility.

These attitudes may seem to us excessively narrow, and so perhaps they are. But they represented for Ascham and his contemporaries a reasonable response to behavior that threatened a social fabric already worn thin by the religious and political reversals through which they had lived. Because attitudes like these grew out of a genuine experience, they were voiced with extraordinary confidence. Ascham stands firmly on the rock of achieved selfhood. He possesses an integrity of being that gives authority to his pronouncements—an authority that must have weighed heavily on young men who had no comparable sense of themselves. We should not, however, attribute too much to Ascham alone. His self-assurance reflects that of his generation. One hears the same steady, confident note in Burghley's letter to Harington or in the letter that Sir Henry Sidney wrote his son Philip. The prodigals knew that patriarchal voice thoroughly and could imitate it to perfection. Gascoigne's Gnomaticus, Lyly's Eubulus, Sidney's Evarchus, or the father in Lodge's *Alarm against Usurers* all share Ascham's solidity. But their creators did not. However charming or graceful, the young men always give the impression that they are striking a pose, and that, of course, is one reason why their various repentances have not been taken seriously. They never seem quite sure who they are. If Gascoigne was something less of a poseur than his successors, it is perhaps because he came of age in the turbulent fifties rather than in the tranquil seventies. The pressures he knew were more like those that formed Ascham, Burghley, and Sir Henry Sidney. But even he was enough younger than these establishers and defenders of order to have developed a romantic and rebellious side that required decisive excision. His intermediate position, between two generations, made him both the first Elizabethan prodigal and one of the most uncompromising of the mid-century enemies of prodigality.

4
Lyly

In 1595, seventeen years after *Euphues* established his reputation, a decade after Elizabeth advised him to "aim all his courses at the Revels," John Lyly acknowledged defeat. "If your sacred Majesty think me unworthy," he wrote the Queen, "and that, after ten years tempest, [I] must at the Court suffer shipwreck of my times, my hopes, and my wits, vouchsafe in your never erring judgment some plank or rafter to waft me into a country, where, in my sad and settled devotion, I may in every corner of a thatched cottage write prayers instead of plays—prayers for your long and prosperous life—and a repentance that I have played the fool so long and yet live." Lyly's "if" suggests that he had yet to reach the dead end of despair. It was, however, not far off. Two years later, in a petition to the Queen's principal secretary, Sir Robert Cecil, Lyly renewed his plea for relief, though now with no sense that the disappointment of his courtly ambition might be avoided. "I hope I shall not be used worse than an old horse who after service done hath his shoes pulled off and turned to grass, not suffered to starve in the stable. I will cast my wits in a new mold . . . for I find it folly that one foot being in the grave, I should have the other on the stage." But, plank or pasturage, relief was denied. "Thirteen years your Highness's servant," he wrote the next year, "but yet nothing."[1] And nothing it remained until his death in 1606, three years after Elizabeth's.

Lyly's repentance, unlike Gascoigne's, does not even pretend to derive from a fear that his work may have misled his audience. Poetry failed him in a more tangible way. Since leaving the university, he had entertained the Court and depended on it for preferment, but his hopes were left unfulfilled. He learned that to expend wit in the making of stories and plays was wasteful folly; it procured nothing. Here then is the pattern of prodigality reduced to its bare economic essentials.

But that pattern had figured significantly in Lyly's career long before neglect moved him to despair. In *Euphues* he created the most imitated avatar of prodigality to appear in sixteenth-century England. What, it is often asked, made this book so extraordinarily popular? Style is the usual answer, the wittily patterned artifice of Lyly's prose. And the usual answer is right, at least in part. But there was more to the appeal of *Euphues* than style. Strange as it may now seem, Lyly's contemporaries were as much taken by the plot, the protagonist, and the moral attitude of *Euphues* as by its Euphuism. Not until Harvey's attack in 1593 did "Euphues" begin to assume its modern connotation as a byword for Lyly's rhetorical manner as distinct from the experience and moral stance of his protagonist[2]—and by 1593 the Euphuistic fashion had largely passed. The six fictions, written prior to that date, which refer explicitly to Euphues, testify to a very different interest.[3] Only one speaks at any length of Euphues' style, and then to reject it as "sauced with a little suspicion of flattery."[4] And only three imitate it. But all six identify Euphues as an antiromantic moralist, "constant in reprehending vanities in love,"[5] and most remember that he came to sagacity by way of error and repentance. The vain futility of courtly delights, as Lodge recalls in *Euphues' Shadow*, "made Euphues repent the prime of his youth misspent in folly and virtuously end the winter of his age in Silixsedra."[6] The image of the former prodigal sententiously edifying the youth of England from his melancholy cell on Silixsedra seems to have particularly struck these writers, for they come back to it again and again. Not all agree with Euphues' opinions—Greene in *Menaphon: Camillo's Alarm to Slumbering Euphues* and John Dickenson in the later *Arisbas: Euphues Amidst his Slumbers* (1594) both defend love against Euphues' attacks—but they do all recognize those opinions as characteristic of Lyly's hero. Furthermore, imitation—imitation of the Euphuistic experience as well as the Euphuistic morality—was at least as common a response as disagreement, and often the imitation was quite open. Rich, for example, says of his *Don Simonides* that "under these clouds of feigned histories . . . you may find the anatomy of wanton youth, seasoned with over-late repentance,"[7] a clear allusion to *The Anatomy of Wit*; and Lodge, still more openly, declares that in his *Euphues' Shadow* he "limn[ed] out under the figure of Philamis the fortunes of Euphues, wherein you shall see that young men's first wits are like April dews which breed more unwholesome weeds than profitable flowers."[8] When we regret, as modern critics often do, *Euphues'* "deficiency of characterization and action," we miss what its first readers found most evident.[9] As a character, Euphues stirred their imaginations as forcefully as any character in modern fiction has stirred ours. Euphues' clever way with words was, of course, one expression of his character and did some of the stirring; the mistake of modern criticism has been to give it credit for doing all.

A sixteenth-century clergyman's remark on the biblical prodigal might be applied to the way some early readers took *Euphues*. "Each several man," he writes, "should be another's looking-glass, but this man is a spectacle in the theater of this world for all men to look upon. . . . We are prone to pattern this prodigal person in his preposterous and perverse affections and we lively bear his image. . . . This poetical fiction fitteth us."[10] I would suggest that the young, humanistically educated men of courtly and literary pretension who came to London in the late 1570's found this looking-glass best set out in Lyly's version of the story of prodigality. Numerous imitations by men like Gosson, Saker, Melbancke, Rich, Lodge, and Greene, many of which claim to shadow their author's own experience, seem to support this suggestion. Lyly's was evidently the poetical fiction that most nearly fit them. And the image was no less applicable for being, as Lyly confessed in *Euphues and his England,* itself a portrait of its author.[11] Defining and dramatizing the self was Lyly's intent. In giving a fictional design to his own life, he apparently seized on much of what seemed most worth emphasizing in theirs, whether they measured that worth in terms of accuracy and sincerity or in terms of self-promotional effect. Nor was the appeal of the image lessened by what today seems most obvious: Euphues' unpleasantness. We find it hard to believe that anyone could ever have admitted, much less cultivated, a likeness to him. That Lyly and his contemporaries failed to notice the unsympathetic side of their chosen model is one of the best clues to the dilemma of their generation.

What is the nature of the Euphuistic identity that these young men were so prone to follow? We notice first that it bears clearly the mark of its lineage—its descent from mid-century humanism. Like *The Schoolmaster* or *The Glass of Government*, the first part of *Euphues* anatomizes wit; like Gascoigne's, Lyly's hero is an overly bright prodigal. Euphues' name and attributes come from Ascham and the names of Eubulus and Philautus from the education drama, which also furnished Lyly his plot with its opening rejection of good advice and its conclusion in repentance.[12] Even Lyly's style has a respectable, schoolmasterly source, the Oxford lectures of William Rainolds, and, through Rainolds, Cicero.[13] Moreover, the book is sprinkled with Ciceronian sentences and bulked out with translations (though unacknowledged) from Ovid and Plutarch. Lyly could hardly have used what he had been taught more systematically. Yet, despite its seeming eagerness to reassert the content of the humanist curriculum and to reemploy the humanist didactic method, *The Anatomy of Wit* covertly and perhaps unconsciously undermines both.

All the most remarkable changes Lyly made in the fiction of the prodigal son testify to his disruptive interest in those courtly manners and Italianate customs that Ascham had disdained. *Euphues* is set not in an inn of questionable repute but in an elegant salon; its leading lady is not a common trull but the well-bred daughter of "one of the chief governors of the city"; the entertainment is not gambling but the fashionable Italian *dubii d'amore*. More significant still, Lyly alters the definition of wit. For Gascoigne, Ascham, and the earlier pedagogical writers, a quick wit meant a quick memory, the most useful intellectual quality in an educational system that put such emphasis on getting one's lessons by heart. For Lyly, wit resides rather in the tongue than in the memory. Wit is the skill at repartee required for success in the sophisticated, courtly *conversazione*: readiness, eloquence, and aptness of response. Euphues, we are told, "gave himself almost to nothing but practising of those things commonly which are incident to these sharp wits—fine phrases, smooth quipping, merry taunting, using jesting without mean, and abusing mirth without measure" (10).

Of itself this proves no irrevocable truancy. Italianate manners and courtly wit are, after all, the stated objects of Lyly's satire. Even if we detect an excessive delight in his portrayal of that which he pretends to correct, it hardly distinguishes him from the schoolmaster dramatists who were titillated by the wantonness they condemned. The satirists of the 1590's recognized this common human paradox when they made envy the chief motive force of their malcontent personae. In *Euphues,* however, the contradiction between the acknowledged and the unacknowledged intent comes closer to the surface. In the opening paragraph Lyly makes the startling admission that not only is the finest wit likely to be the most wicked but that this very imperfection is the secret of its attraction.

As therefore the sweetest rose hath his prickle, the finest velvet his brack, the fairest flour his bran, so the sharpest wit hath his wanton will and the holiest head his wicked way. And true it is that some men write, and most men believe, that in all perfect shapes a blemish bringeth rather a liking every way to the eyes than a loathing any way to the mind. Venus had her mole in her cheek which made her more amiable; Helen her scar on her chin which Paris called cos amoris, *the whetstone of love; Aristippus his wart, Lycurgus his wen.* (10)

When an author begins by admitting that, though his anatomy uncover vicious imperfections, they may be regarded as a *cos amoris,* his satire is disarmed and his doubleness of intent made too apparent to be ignored. Moreover, in this case, the witty rhetorical patterns on which the author's own claim to the attention of his audience so largely depends derive from the discovery (and on occasion from the manufacture) of imperfection. For Lyly's style to use them, the sweetest rose must have his prickle, the finest velvet his brack. Whatever he may claim to the contrary, Lyly necessarily delights in the world's imperfection. Without it there would be no antithesis, and without antithesis there would be no Euphuism.[14]

We can perhaps best appreciate Lyly's ambivalence by looking at a particular problem. Take, for example, the question of experience. The humanist position, championed early in the century by Lyly's grandfather, was, as Erasmus so flatly put it, that "experience is the common schoolhouse of fools and ill men."[15] Colet and William Lily began St. Paul's School, and Erasmus and Lily wrote its first textbook with the idea that their age could be reformed by learning and imitating the example of antiquity. A faith in the moral effect of exempla was the trait most characteristic of the movement they represent. What happens to that faith in *Euphues*? It is subject to such questioning that *The Anatomy of Wit* has been described as "a book celebrating experience."[16] The first words of Euphues' pedagogical treatise, "Euphues and his Ephebus," do sound like a direct answer to Erasmus. "It is commonly said, yet I do think it a common lie, that experience is the mistress of fools; for in my opinion they be most fools that want it" (111). But, seen from another point of view, Euphues' position appears no different from that of Gnomaticus who in *The Glass of Government* had suggested that the prodigals might, as a last resort, be left to experience the world without the mediation of precept and example. Euphues asserts only that one *may* learn, as he did, from experience. His treatise, however, shows that by starting early enough (with Walter Shandy he suggests beginning at the moment of procreation) a youth may be prevented from having to rely on the painful lessons of experience. He writes, not in praise of experience, but "to the intent . . . that all young gentlemen might shun my former looseness" (113).

But the ambivalence continues as Lyly's didactic pretensions are undone by his artistic success in the creation of character. Euphues and Lucilla make nonsense of talk about nurture. Both discover that the exemplary patterns of behavior culled from antiquity are amoral in their effect. Those patterns are mirrors in which we see ourselves with unequaled clarity. But though they advance us in self-knowledge, they do nothing to increase our moral self-control. However Euphues and Lucilla got to be what they are, it is clear that nothing, certainly no packaged wisdom, has the strength to divert them from their fated course. In describing their consistency we do not need to invoke the strange formulations of Renaissance psychology, the irrationalities of humor adjust or the absolute disjunction of *ethos* and *pathos*. Euphues and Lucilla appear as coherent to us now as they must have to their original audience.

Though Lucilla is transformed by passion, there has been ample warning that she felt uncomfortable in the role of fiancée to the tiresomely respectable Philautus. Her uncivil reception of Euphues, introduced as Philautus's friend, marks a preliminary rebellion against the conventions of that role. Euphues does not miss the meaning of her action; her disdain provokes and excites him. In the first interview they have alone, she shows herself the equal of Cressida at stirring the sexual appetite of her victim. Like Shakespeare's heroine, she instinctively knows the art of holding off. She plays tauntingly with temptation, making sexual innuendoes more overt than anything the stiffly prudish Euphues would have dared. Her effect on him is much that which Cressida has on Troilus. "Euphues was brought into a great quandary and as it were a cold shivering to hear this new kind of kindness, such sweet meat, such sour sauce, such fair words, such faint promises, such hot love, such cold desire, such certain hope, such sudden change" (65). Lucilla clearly finds her true self in this role which she plays so brilliantly. Her succeeding development, her lust for Curio and her tragic end, is more briefly sketched but follows naturally from what we already know of her.

In the character of Euphues, Lyly created one of the most consistently unsympathetic figures in English literature. Whether as prodigal or as precisian, complacent self-satisfaction is the constant base of his character. The example of the schoolmaster dramatists and the classical moralists may have dictated the choice of self-love as the prodigal's motivating flaw, but Lyly had too firm a conception of the character of Euphues to suppose that his moral reformation would change more than the local expression of his enduring *philautia*. Egotism, not the passion of youth, led to his rejection of Eubulus' advice. He stood "in his own light," deeming "no penny good silver but his own" (25). Likewise, he chose his friend out of self-love. "By so much the more I make myself sure to have Philautus, by how much the more I view in him the lively image of Euphues" (29). Not even his love was motivated by the charms of his beloved. He was initially provoked by Lucilla's failure to notice him and was led on by her reversal to flattering attention. The spur to his reformation was a sudden shock to his self-esteem, the discovery that he too might be jilted, and for the unprepossessing Curio at that. He begins at once on the course that will complete his alienation from our esteem by self-righteously lecturing Lucilla on inconstancy, a failing of which he was so recently guilty. Remorse and self-incrimination play a small part in the solitary lament which follows. He refuses to see his own treachery imaged in Lucilla's. "I had thought that women had been as we men, that is, true, faithful, zealous, constant; but I perceive they be rather woe unto men by their falsehood, jealousy, inconstancy" (84). His "Cooling Card for Philautus and All Fond Lovers" is no more fatuously inappropriate than the blindly condescending "Certain Letters" which he writes. He reproves Philautus, whose greatest transgression is having let himself be betrayed by Euphues; corrects Alcius, a young prodigal; and impudently chides Botonio and Eubulus, the one for regretting his exile, the other for lamenting the death of his daughter. This last impresses particularly as insensitive nonsense, as does his letter to Philautus on the death of Lucilla. Philautus's sorrow is far more attractive than Euphues' prudish disdain. He neglects to remember that Lucilla was the woman for whom he betrayed the friend he now so self-righteously corrects. Euphues knows nothing of positive goodness; his virtue is wholly negative. To his friend Livia he writes that "to reprove sin is the sign of true honor, to renounce it the part of honesty . . . for they say to abstain from pleasure is the chiefest piety; and I think in court to refrain from vice is no little virtue" (180). The fact that the "they" in question is Cicero does little to make this sentiment more attractive, though it may have masked its want of charity from a classicist.[17] Far from renewing the humanist tradition through his borrowing from it, Lyly reveals the poverty to which it had been reduced. Reproving and renouncing, abstaining and refraining are all that Euphues' sources can show him in the way of virtue.

Out of the most narrowly repressive principles of mid-century humanism, Lyly has created a strikingly consistent character, a monstrous prig. If his creation has not received all the praise it deserves, it is perhaps because readers suspect Lyly of not knowing what he was doing. They are probably right. Without a trace of irony he offers the reformed Euphues for our admiration and emulation. The narrator, who in the early pages never tired of undercutting the pretensions of Euphues, seems by the end of the book to have merged with him, leaving us uncomfortably opposed to both with only the sanction of our own subjective feelings, feelings that were apparently not shared by Lyly's first readers. There was, of course, to be a reaction, as titles like *Camilla's Alarm to Slumbering Euphues* (1589) or *Euphues Amidst His Slumbers* (1594) indicate, and Lyly himself was to get the reaction started with his sequel to *The Anatomy of Wit*. But in the years immediately following the publication of the first *Euphues*, the priggishness seems to have gone unnoticed. And here is the real mystery. Why was such an unattractive character so attractive to the younger Elizabethans? If we can answer that, we will have gone a long way toward understanding them.

First we should admit that it was not Euphues' self-conceit that they most eagerly imitated, but something of it almost inevitably crept in. We find, for example, Austen Saker's Narbonus complacently warning his former companions of the dangers of the court that he has so recently left, or Stephen Gosson's Phialo superciliously lecturing a friend on how to lecture a friend.[18] Self-conceit was difficult to avoid because their books were advertisements for themselves. "Employ me," they say, "I am properly disillusioned. Dangerous youth is safely behind me, and here are its fruits, repentence and virtuous admonition." This quality of self-advertisement makes irrelevent a complaint like Sidney's about the style of *Euphues*. Of course its strings of similes are unpersuasive. Such criticism mistakes the rhetorical objective. The Euphuists were trying less to sell ideas (their ideas were, after all, commonplaces usually chosen to reflect the prejudices of their audience) than to sell themselves. They displayed wit and, at the same time, showed by the plot of their story a critical awareness of the danger of wit. They thus made a simultaneous claim to wit and wisdom. But, in doing so, they could hardly avoid that mixture of petulant insolence and learned pride which Smollett two centuries later defined as priggishness.[19]

Euphues was attractive to young men of Lyly's age in part because they thought he would be attractive to their elders. Gosson, Saker, Brian Melbancke, and Barnabe Rich all adopt Lyly's notion that experience justifies the warnings of age, particularly the warning against the lascivious and effeminate pleasure of love. Like Euphues, Saker's Narbonus, Rich's Don Simonides, and Melbancke's Philotimus learn to their cost the fickleness of woman, and we are meant to see that the author shared the lesson. "But some," Saker tells us, "will imagine me to have been in love for putting here this name of lust, but rather they may think me to have lived by the loss that have been lured so much to my own liberty" (Sig. Aiii). He does not deny that he has been in love, but he does insist on his disillusionment. And love, though the most frequent, is not the only folly these prodigals learn to regret. Travel, military adventure, courtly fashion, and financial imprudence all yield to the corrosive rust of experience. Even play-making fits into the pattern of youthful rebellion. In *The School of Abuse* Gosson assumes the Euphuistic pose (and Euphues' style) to condemn his former profession of dramatist. "After wits are even best; burnt children dread the fire. I have seen that which you behold, and I shun that which you frequent."[20] We know that Gosson was trying to please his elders; the Mayor and Aldermen of London commissioned *The School of Abuse*.[21] But even where the pressure was less direct, paternal expectation compelled these writers to portray youth as a period of instructive failure. And, whether they produced autobiographical fiction or Gosson's sort of autobiographical fact, *Euphues* showed them how to do it.

They hadn't, however, only their elders in mind. Lyly addresses his "very good friends the gentlemen scholars of Oxford," Saker "the gentlemen readers," Gosson the "literarum studiosis in Oxoniensi academia," Rich "the noble gentlemen of England," Melbancke "my very friends, the gentlemen students in the Inns of Court and Chancery and the University of

Cambridge." Each must cope with a complex rhetorical occasion, a double audience with contradictory interests. Most early Euphuistic fiction is, as a result, like a three-way conversation. One young man admonishes another while an old man listens, and this situation makes inevitable the attitudinizing that in *Euphues* takes the form of priggishness. To the old man the speaker must seem to say, "My unfortunate experience has made me share your point of view. I know the world and its dangers and can join you in warning against them." Or, as Gosson puts it in *The School of Abuse*, "He that hath been shook with a fierce ague giveth good counsel to his friends when he is well."[22] But if he does not wish to drive away his friends, he must mix more attractive matter with his advice. To them he says, "I warn against experience, but look how cleverly I do it and how much of it I have had." This divided audience explains the obsessive concern with pleasure *and* profit. The spider requires his poison as well as the bee his honey. Thus in *The Ephemerides of Phialo*, Gosson's surrogate must at once please Philotimo, the amorous young courtier, and Jeraldi, the old moralist. The mark of his success is that in the end the two join "to procure some friendship for Phialo in the Court"—a model of the success Gosson and the rest hoped would be theirs.

Gosson, at least, was not to be disappointed, though Sir Philip Sidney, the young man to whom both *The School of Abuse* and *The Ephemerides* were dedicated, scorned him for his labor.[23] Gosson alienated his poetically inclined contemporaries, but his attack on the stage set him in the way of preferment. He finished his days as the prosperous rector of St. Botolph's, one of the best livings in London.[24] Lyly, who was born in the same year as Gosson, who studied at the same Canterbury school, and who imitated the rhetorical tricks of the same Oxford lecturer, but whose work pleased his contemporaries more than his elders, ended life as a genteel beggar. The contrast between these two careers reveals how much was at stake in the Euphuists' balancing act. They risked either the scorn of their fellows or the disapprobation of those in power. The first no doubt meant a loss of self-esteem, a sense that one had turned coat and gone over to the enemy; the other, a loss of income.

Euphues mirrors the division in Lyly's audience. Like the prodigal generation, the book is torn by opposite and irreconcilable tendencies. It maintains the content and didactic method of mid-century humanism. It takes over the story of the prodigal son and repeats the expected themes, the warning against women, against love, against travel, and so on. It incorporates a translation of one of the primary sources of humanistic pedagogy, Plutarch's treatise on the education of children, which includes mention of the ideal union of wit and wisdom, nurture and nature, the active and the contemplative lives. But, like the freshest colors that soonest fade, this world, as Lyly develops it, engenders its own opposite. Analytic wit allows no synthesizing wisdom. Fully created nature defies nurture. And the contempt of the world implicit in the prodigal son plays expands to destroy the active life. Euphues, Phialo, Narbonus, Don Simonides, and Philotimus remain, if not specifically contemplatives, lonely and disillusioned outsiders. I suspect their creators left them that way because they were unable to imagine their own place in society. On whose terms were they to enter? Their own or their fathers'? Caught between dependence and independence, they found themselves shut off from the active life, however much they may have wished to embrace it.

Like the usual prodigal son story, the history of the prodigal generation falls into three phases: admonition, rebellion, and repentance. The first centers on *The Anatomy of Wit*. In it the various glasses of government, rocks of regard, schools of abuse, and labyrinths of liberty find their point of convergence. No single book so definitively expresses the next phase, the period of rebellion. Four works do, however, stand out: Lyly's *Euphues and his England*, Greene's *Pandosto*, Lodge's *Rosalind*, and Sidney's New *Arcadia*. Greene, Lodge, and Sidney will preoccupy us in the next several chapters. In the remaining pages of this one, I would like to suggest what Lyly did to Euphues.

The critics who have discussed Lyly in greatest detail disagree about the relation of *The Anatomy of Wit* to its sequel. On the one hand, Albert Feuillerat and Walter Davis have thought the works very different indeed, Davis claiming that the second "is in many ways a complete departure" from the first, and Feuillerat identifying that departure with a transfer of Lyly's primary allegiance from the Protestant humanists to the Italianate courtiers, from Burghley to Oxford.[25] G. K. Hunter, on the other hand, has disputed this biographical explanation and denied that there is enough of a difference between the two parts of *Euphues* to need explaining. *The Anatomy of Wit*, Hunter points out, was not dedicated to Burghley, but to Sir William West, Lord Delaware. Of Delaware not enough is known to speculate about the nature of his influence. Nor is it clear that the viciousness of Oxford's life led him as a patron to prefer licentious writing. As Hunter remarks, Oxford "'commanded' his 'loving friend' Thomas Bedingfield to translate Cardan's *Comfort* into English (1573) and this argues seriousness of mind and sobriety of taste."[26] This successfully weakens Feuillerat's biographical reasoning. It does not of course prove the two works alike, nor does Hunter pretend it should. He argues rather that there can be no significant opposition between *The Anatomy of Wit* and *Euphues and his England* because neither has any definable coherence. Each is a "gallimaufry," a collection of *topoi*, of popular themes, of attitudes adopted one minute to be dropped the next. To prove the two works alike one need only demonstrate, as Hunter does, that they discuss similar subjects in a similar style, using a similar fiction, that of the prodigal son. Looking any closer at the way these subjects or that fiction is handled smacks for Hunter of anachronistic, novel-conditioned criticism.

Hunter's view accounts more adequately than either Feuillerat's or Davis's could for the commonplace and courtesy book quality of both parts of *Euphues*, yet, in my opinion, it is considerably overstated. Though Hunter claims that "we must derive our interpretation from the whole drift of the book," his argument denies that *Euphues* has any such thing. "Drift" implies direction; Hunter allows only a swirling movement in place. Yet despite the admittedly frequent eddies and countercurrents, most readers do recognize that each version has its own drift and that the drift of *Euphues and his England* opposes that of its predecessor. One is addressed to gentlemen scholars, the other to ladies and gentlewomen; one claims to be a moral treatise, the other a plaything; one satirizes women and love, the other praises both. As Lyly wrote in the Epistle Dedicatory to *Euphues and his England,* "Had I not named Euphues, few would have thought it had been Euphues" (194). And not only is the second *Euphues* unlike the first; it is unlike any prodigal son story we have before encountered. It grants the prodigal at least a partial victory, demonstrating to even his Eubulean counsellor that conventional wisdom must be modified, not merely endorsed, by experience.

In *Euphues and his England,* Philautus plays the prodigal and Euphues takes the role unhappiness won him of moral instructor. His lesson, which occupies the first of the book's three parts, does move, as Hunter says, "somewhat jerkily" from topic to topic, as Lyly exhausts first one and then another page of his commonplace book; but plot governs the underlying drift, for Euphues' lesson takes the form of a narrative, a prodigal son story, or rather two prodigal son stories in one, and both reveal a new skepticism about humanistic morality. Euphues begins with the story of Callimachus, whose father, "the lewd usurer" Cassander, dies, leaving his son only a legacy of good advice. Callimachus naturally rebels and sets out to see the world. On his way he meets a hermit living in an ascetic paradise where cat and mouse play at peace together. Unknown to Callimachus, the hermit is his uncle, the twin brother of his father, in whose keeping his fortune has secretly been left. The hermit tries to dissuade him from travel by telling the second prodigal son story, his own. He and his brother, twins of opposite nature though of identical nurture, each inherited a share of their father's wealth. He wasted his part in travel and riotous living, while his brother prudently stayed at home and got richer and richer. The hermit draws the obvious moral, "Then, my good Callimachus, record with thyself the inconveniences that come by travelling" (219). Callimachus rejects his advice, arguing much as Euphues did in *The Anatomy of Wit* that because experience has brought suffering to some it need not do so to him. But of course it does. After much travel he returns to the hermit's cell to confess, "I find too late, yet at length, that in age there is a certain foresight which youth cannot search, and a kind of experience into which unripened years cannot come; so that I must of necessity confess that youth never reineth well but when age holdeth the bridle" (224-225). Euphues concludes by turning from parable to precept. "Be not lavish of thy tongue," he warns Philautus. "Everyone that shaketh thee by the hand is not joined to thee in heart. . . . Be not quarrelous for every light occasion. . . . Beware thou fall not into the snares of love" (226)—the same advice item for item that Eubulus gave him, that the usurous father gave Callimachus, and that any Elizabethan schoolboy was likely to have encountered in Isocrates' *Ad Demonicum*, if he had not already heard it from his father.

This episode remains firmly attached to the humanistic ethos. Both Euphues' tale of Callimachus and the hermit's tale of himself end with the usual overthrow of prodigality, but in both there is an uncharacteristic reluctance to believe that admonition can have any effect. The father does not trust Callimachus with his inheritance despite the counsel he has given him, and the uncle admits, "But why go I about to dissuade thee from that which I myself followed, or to persuade thee to that which thou thyself fliest? My gray hairs are like unto a white frost, thy red blood not unlike a hot fire; so that it cannot be that either thou shouldst follow my counsel or I allow thy conditions" (221). Euphues, speaking to Philautus, echoes him, "I well believe thou rememberest nothing that may do thee good nor forgettest anything which can do thee harm" (229). Furthermore, the hermit's story demonstrates with almost scientific rigor that nature resists nurture. "We were nursed both with one teat," he says of himself and his twin, "where my brother sucked a desire of thrift, and I of theft. . . . So one womb nourished contrary wits and one milk divers manners; which argueth something in nature, I know not what, to be marvellous, I dare not say monstrous" (215-216). Marvelous or monstrous, it is something that would hardly please a humanist.

That humanist would have been no better pleased by the opposition, in both stories, of avarice and prodigality—a paradigm more suggestive of Horace, Terence, or their Italian imitators than of the schoolmaster dramatists.[27] Instead of the usual dialectic of virtue and vice, Euphues' exempla present opposed extremes, with the inevitable suggestion that virtue is to be found not with one or the other, but somewhere in between. The avaricious father is as little to be imitated as his prodigal son. And his precepts so resemble those of Euphues and the hermit that we necessarily brand the morality that all three represent as a miserly tradition.

Wisdom is great wealth. Sparing is good getting. . . . Put no more clothes on thy back than will expel cold, neither any more meat in thy belly than may quench hunger. . . . Enter not into bands, no, not for thy best friends; he that payeth another man's debt seeketh his own decay. . . . Be not hasty to marry. It is better to have one plough going than two cradles; and more profit to have a barn filled than a bed. . . . Be not too lavish in giving alms. . . . And he that cannot follow good counsel never can get commodity. (209-210)

The strict rational prudence of Isocrates and his humanist imitators is shown to verge on uncharitable money grasping. Virtue resides as little with it as with prodigality, and prodigality has at least the advantage of leading to repentance, while avarice leads only to a mean old age and a sordid death.

Euphues has unconsciously posed a dilemma. The next episode, still another prodigal son story, begins to find a way out of it. Again Lyly raids his commonplace book—in this section Hunter notices topics ranging from "the mystery of kingship" to "wine—pro and contra"—but again plot, however jerky its progress, does define a recognizable drift. The story of Fidus, the retired courtier turned beekeeper whom Euphues and Philautus meet on the road to London, opens as usual with a scene of advice given and rejected. The young Fidus, newly arrived at court, is admonished by a grave friend who perceives in him, just as Eubulus, Euphues, and the hermit perceived in the young men they advised, a good wit but a wanton will. And if this friend's allowance of riding, running at the tilt, and reveling seem to owe more to the Italian *Book of the Courtier* than to humanistic pedagogical treatises, the warning against love and women with which he concludes is just what we have come to expect. Fidus's reception of this misogynist counsel also runs true to course. "I gave him great thanks—and glad I was we were parted. For his putting love into my mind was like the throwing of bugloss into wine: which increaseth in him that drinketh it a desire of lust" (250). Unlike Euphues, who in his examples moved rapidly from the disobedient departure to the penitent return, only mentioning the years of prodigality, Fidus lingers nostalgically over each detail of the progress of his love, repeating conversations, *questioni d'amore*, and melancholy soliloquies. Though his love proves ultimately unhappy, leading him, like Euphues and the prodigal hermit, to retire from the world, his beloved is not unfaithful. Iffida is, in fact, the first honest woman we have met. Nor does Fidus tell his tale as a warning to Philautus. Theirs is not the usual relationship of graybeard moralist to young scapegrace. The old lover rather reminisces for the benefit of a young initiate. "Well, God grant Philautus better success than I had" (273). Many of the fictions of the first phase of Elizabethan prodigality, including its centerpiece, *The Anatomy of Wit*, instruct the reader in the mysteries of polite courtship—and that instruction contributed mightily to their success—but this is the first to admit it.

The tales of the hermit, of Callimachus, and of Fidus constitute the opening movement of *Euphues and his England*. The first two set avarice against prodigality; the third explores the bittersweet of prodigal love. The story to which they are prologue takes away the bitter and leaves only the sweet. It thus breaks the confines of humanistic admonition, confines which, with some stretching, could still have accommodated the unrepentant, but unhappy Fidus. If he did not draw the usual moral from his story, Euphues easily could and, once he and Philautus were on the road again, did. Philautus's experience, however, disproves the usual warnings, confirming our impression of significant drift.

Philautus begins by imitating his prodigal predecessors. He rejects traditional wisdom and gives himself up to love. Like Fidus's Iffida, his Camilla is a model of faithful virtue; and, like Iffida, she is faithful to someone else. He tries to win her by magic and by the magic of rhetoric, and, when all fails, he decides to sicken and die. He regrets having estranged Euphues and recalls his advice. "Now, now, Euphues, I see what it is to want a friend, and what it is to lose one; thy words are come to pass, which once I thought thou spakest in sport, now I find them as a prophecy" (362). Normally this would be the prelude to Philautus's retirement from the world. But here the story takes a new and more obliging direction. To replace his rose, Philautus is offered a violet, Mistress Francis. "Be merry, gentleman; at this time of the year a violet is better than a rose" (383). Philautus debates the necessity of lasting faith even to a hopeless love, prevaricates, and ends by marrying his English violet. Here then prodigality is not punished, but rewarded, if not with what it at first desired, at least with something almost as good. Philautus has been allowed to stray rather far from the narrow path of virtue, particularly in his Italianate recourse to necromantic intrigue, without undue suffering. This is no longer the dangerous world where any false step was irretrievable. The women in England are virtuous, the men loyal. Even the Italian magician turns out to be a benign philosopher. The palpable evil of *The Glass of Government* and *The Anatomy of Wit* has been dispelled. In England one can muddle through with impunity.

These further adventures of Euphues and Philautus test humanistic precept against the reality of contemporary England. *The Anatomy of Wit* had been set in a semiallegorical Naples which stood at once for the Italy against which Ascham had railed and the Italianate English metropolis. Until the mention of Elizabeth in the final pages, its time had been no more definite. It began like an old tale. "There dwelt in Athens a young gentleman of great patrimony and of so comely a personage" (10). *Euphues and his England* insists on its own actuality. It begins, "Euphues, having gotten all things necessary for his voyage into England, accompanied only with Philautus, took shipping the first of December, 1579, by our English computation" (205). It seems at moments almost to have been written as it was being lived. "To make short, the winds were so favorable, the mariners so skilful, the way so short, that I fear me they will land before I can describe the manner how—and therefore suppose them now in Dover town" (231). In this contemporary setting even Euphues discovers that his teaching must be modified. He recants his "Cooling Card" and advises Philautus to marry. The irrelevance of his preconceived morality is mirrored in the inadequacy of his geography, based as it is on the same kind of classical sources. On the boat he concludes his moral lesson by edifying his traveling companions with a description of England, but his humanistic Baedeker, Caesar's *Gallic Wars,* is as preposterously out of date as his misogynism. He gets the orientation of the island wrong and informs his listeners that the "coin they use is either brass or else iron rings," and that "all the Britains do dye themselves with woad, which setteth a bluish color upon them" (227-228). Experience teaches him that *De Bello Gallico* works no better as a travel guide than Ovid's *Remedia Amoris* did as an introduction to love. In a letter sent to Livia from his cell on Mount Silixsedra, he corrects his misconceptions about the geography and manners of Britain, basing his revised report on the very recent *Description of England* (1577) by William Harrison. Philautus's experiences in England bring his misogynism up to date.

Euphues is forced to change his ideas as no other Eubulean sage ever was. He does not, however, change enough. He remains an alien figure in England. He is respected; his company is sought; his advice requested; but he is, nevertheless, an outsider. At the dinner party at Lady Flavia's all the guests are paired, Surius with Camilla, Philautus with Mistress Francis, even the aging hostess with the supernumerary Martius. Only Euphues, who is chosen to judge their debate on love, remains unmated. And he concludes against them all. "Great hold there hath been who should prove his love best, when in my opinion there is none good" (405). His judgment is not so much wrong as irrelevant. He would ground love wholly upon "time, reason, favor, and virtue," ignoring the irrational passion which is an inevitable ingredient of love, even for the most virtous of English women, Camilla. Again in his debate with Philautus, Euphues fails to strike the right note, the note that might make him part of that harmonious English chorus he so much admires. He praises love, renouncing his former satire, but it is the wrong kind, chaste spiritual love, not the love that realizes itself in a fruitful marriage. The narrator, for once unequivocally on the side of Philautus, agrees in defending this typically English resolution of the conflict of passion and reason. "I must needs conclude with Philautus, though I should cavil with Euphues, that the end of love is the full fruition of the party beloved" (382).

Like Jacques, another reformed prodigal turned moralist, Euphues has no place in the comic world of love and marriage. He blesses the newlyweds and gives them a little more good advice culled from the *Conjugal Precepts* of Plutarch. Then, just as Jacques quit the regenerated world of *As You Like It* to join the convertite Duke Frederick, Euphues withdraws to his cell on Mount Silixsedra, its "seat of flint" figuring the hardness of his doctrine. He and his humanistic morality are for other than the dancing measures of England in 1580.

What accounts for the extraordinary change in Lyly's fiction? The dedication of *Euphues and his England* to the Earl of Oxford provides, as Feuillerat realized, an important clue. If the particular tastes of Oxford and his circle did not shape the second *Euphues* to quite the extent that Feuillerat thought, Lyly's association with Oxford did at least decide the orientation of his career, and his book reflects that orientation. Like *The Anatomy of Wit*, *Euphues and his England* reaches out for preferment. But where Lyly before thought preferment could be had only by repenting passion and the literature that expresses it, he now allows passion, and thus by extension allows literature. Ambition's aim was still the court, but by the time he wrote *Euphues and his England*, Lyly saw a possibility of realizing ambition as a writer. Prodigal son stories of the stricter sort generally advertise themselves as the unique product of youthful folly. The author, they claim, will now turn to graver subjects. And that is, in fact, what Gascoigne, Whetstone, Rich, and Gosson did, while Saker and Melbancke stopped writing altogether.[28] Lyly, with the help of Oxford, took another road. Within a few years we find him producing comedies for the court under Oxford's patronage, and for almost a decade he was the most popular court dramatist. But this hopeful development did not have a happy ending. By the early 1590's, he had lost his audience, and in 1595 came the first of the pleading epistles to Elizabeth and Cecil, admitting failure and announcing literary repentance.

In those letters we hear once again the voice of Euphues, witty though repentant. It was a role that Lyly never wholly abandoned. He claimed it not only in the Epistle Dedicatory to *Euphues and his England,* but also in the letter he prefixed to Thomas Watson's *Hekatompathia* (1582). "The repeating of love," he wrote, "wrought in me a remembrance of liking, but searching the very veins of my heart, I could find nothing but a broad scar where I left a deep wound. . . . Whereby I noted that young swans are gray and the old white, young trees tender and the old tough, young men amorous and growing in years either wiser or warier."[29] Despite his portrayal of Philautus's success, Lyly continued to wear the mask of disillusionment. Like Euphues, he was the old swan, the old tree, the old man wiser and warier, kept by experience from joining the celebration that he heralded. Brought up under the Old Law, he could not accept grace.

5
Greene

No one will be surprised to find prodigality linked with the name of Robert Greene. Who can forget Harvey's account of his riotous life and miserable death, the penury, the loneliness, the pitiful plea for a cup of Malmsey wine?[1] Even the printer of Greene's last work saw him as a prodigal. "And forasmuch as the purest glass is the most brickle, the finest lawn the soonest stained, the highest oak the most subject to the wind, and the quickest wit the most easily won to folly, I doubt not but you will with regard forget his follies and, like to the bee, gather honey out of [his] good counsels."[2] This passage carries us from Harvey's colored facts into the realm of Euphuistic fiction. The language is Lyly's; the figure described a latter-day Euphues, quick witted, easily won to folly, transformed by repentance into a good counsellor.

Neither Harvey nor the printer invented the identification of Greene with the prodigal. Greene himself discovered and publicized this myth, and in so doing he replaced Euphues as the most popular Elizabethan representative of the type. But, unlike Euphues', Greene's was a particularly literary prodigality. He did of course make much of his dissolute life, his abandonment of his wife and his wanton behavior in London, but he regretted still more the vanity of his "amorous pamphlets." Thrice called back from the grave, by Henry Chettle in *Kind-Heart's Dream* (1592), by B. R. in *Greene's News both from Heaven and Hell* (1593), and by John Dickenson in *Greene in Conceit* (1598), he appears always in the guise of the repentant author, prohibited heaven, according to B. R., "for writing of books." But if writing damned him, it also saved him. He was "banished out of [hell] for displaying of conny-catchers." This appraisal of Greene's chances in eternity, borrowed from his own oft repeated judgment of himself, completes the pattern of prodigality. Satire serves an antidote to romance. The former wanton makes amends by warning others of the dangers he has known. Gascoigne did it; Euphues did it; and now Greene does it. But even Greene's admonition has particular application to the literary world. He directs his counsel "to those gentlemen his quondam acquaintance that spend their wits in making plays" (XII, 141).

Greene was more a writer and less a courtier than the other university or inns of court men of his generation. Nothing in his career compares to Lyly's parliamentary service, to the military employment of Gascoigne, Rich, Whetstone, or Saker, to Gosson's advancement in the Church, to Lodge's adventuring, Sidney's work as a diplomat, or Harington's attendance at court. Nor does Greene seem to have written with an eye to preferment. "He made no account," Nashe tells us, "of winning credit by his works. . . . His only care was to have a spell in his purse to conjure up a good cup of wine with at all times."[3] His works did have politically and socially prominent dedicatees, but he seems to have hoped from them no more than money. His real audience was the bookbuying public. As long as that audience patronized romance, it mattered little to Greene that his writing might disqualify him from more respectable employment. This insouciance won him a literary freedom that most of his contemporaries lacked, a freedom that was, however, short-lived. For despite his apparent indifference to the expectations that usually accompanied a humanistic education, he was eventually overtaken by repentance and his abandoned self.

Why is so much Elizabethan fiction autobiographical? Part of the reason is self-advertisement, but part too may be guilt. As Paul Goodman has remarked, "The guilty do not pay attention to the object but only to themselves."[4] Greene's career nicely illustrates this truism. As his guilt increased, so did his attention to himself, until, in one of the most remarkable passages in sixteenth-century fiction, he breaks off his *Groatsworth of Wit* to confess that he and his protagonist are one. "Hereafter suppose me the said Roberto" (XII, 137). And his last work, his *Repentance*, is explicit autobiography. Like Lyly, who identified himself with Euphues but not with Philautus, Greene enters his own fiction only when it records defeat. But before coming home to the guilty self, he went much further than Lyly had in the exploration of a romantic other.

Greene's career began in the shadow of *The Anatomy of Wit.* The style, action, and characters of his first work, *Mamillia: A Mirror or Looking-Glass for the Ladies of England,* are stamped with the likeness of *Euphues.*[5] In its first pages we learn of the correspondence of the heroine, Mamillia, with the moral Florion. Like Euphues, Florion has been deceived in love and, as a result, has abandoned women. His advice to Mamillia closely resembles Euphues' to Livia. "It is a great virtue," he writes, counseling Mamillia to quit the court, "to abstain from pleasure" (II, 37).[6] He warns her of the danger of love, of the fickleness of men, of "the substance of vice with the veil of virtue" (II, 37). She accepts his counsel, retires to her father's home, and bridles her passions with reason.

Such unprodigal docility would have left Lyly and the schoolmaster dramatists with no story to tell. But in Greene's fiction, whatever it may owe to Lyly, no care protects adequately against the perils of love and adverse fortune. Despite her mastery of precept, Mamillia succumbs to a wily deceiver. Greene's story thus suggests a disjunction between precept and experience quite foreign to *Euphues.* In Lyly's novel passion overturns precept and nature upsets nurture, but, if successfully adhered to, precept and nurture would guard one against the dangers of love. In Greene precept and nurture are equally irrelevant, and virtue, however resolute, provides no defense against vice. Virtue and vice are alike pawns in the hand of all-governing fortune, and in some stories fortune dispenses altogether with the instrument of passion, creating disorder by mere natural accident.

Greene's fiction does not, however, lack order. Vicious passion, though beyond effective human control, always meets with punishment and virtue quite often receives some reward. But, if Greene on occasion provides a happy ending, he rarely allows virtue to bring it about. Virtue remains as passive and powerless in victory as in defeat. The inhuman and impersonal force that does arrange accident into orderly patterns is time.

Thus *Pandosto* is subtitled "The Triumph of Time" and the title page of *Menaphon* promises that here "are deciphered the variable effects of fortune, the wonders of love, the triumphs of inconstant time." In both stories an oracle guarantees that random fortune will eventually arrange the characters according to a predetermined pattern. In *Menaphon* the pattern is so obscure that "an old woman attired like a prophetess" comes on for the sole purpose of pointing out that the oracle has been accomplished. Not only are the characters incapable of working out their own happiness, they cannot even recognize it when it has been achieved for them. They are, as Greene often hints, players in a drama whose plot they ignore. In this senseless world where human action has neither significance nor effect, stoic resignation is the prime virtue.

Greene seems, at first at least, unaware of how far he has departed from the humanistic moral tradition which stood behind *Euphues.* Particularly in the earliest of his works, and occasionally even after, he indulges in didactic reflections wholly inappropriate to an action so completely dominated by fortune. He does, however, acknowledge another departure from the tradition of *The Anatomy of Wit* and its misogynous forebears. *Mamillia* openly defends women. It is a work "wherein with perpetual fame the constancy of gentlewomen is canonized and the unjust blasphemies of women's supposed fickleness (breathed out by diverse injurious persons) by manifest examples clearly infringed" (II, 139). Lyly's portrayal of Iffida and Camilla in *Euphues and his England* may have led the way, but Greene seizes on the theme with the eagerness of a man who has found a cause both popular and suited to the kind of fiction he wanted in any case to write—fiction which prizes the feminine virtue of passive resignation in the face of masculine brutality and the ravages of fortune.

As the women's stock goes up, the men's comes down. The typical villain in Greene is a masculine figure of authority, a father or husband, an elder or ruler. This too sets him against Lyly and the writers of prodigal son plays. In the education drama, in Macropedius and Stymmelius and the English writers prior to Gascoigne, the parents were often guilty, but of excessive kindness rather than cruelty. And one older figure, the schoolmaster or good counselor, was always there to represent true wisdom. Similarly in Lyly the elder generation is both sympathetic and wise. Eubulus, Ferardo, the hermit, Fidus's father, and Lady Flavia all stand for positive values, though from the antiromantic Eubulus to the matchmaking Lady Flavia the character of those values changes markedly. Much the same sympathy attaches to the older people in *Mamillia*, but in his succeeding work Greene abandons this benevolent view of authority. A conflict between established, but abusive authority and youth soon comes to occupy the dramatic center of his fiction. Greene found this theme first in the Apocrypha, in the story of Susanna and the Elders, which he embellished with the usual Euphuistic ornaments and presented as the *Mirror of Modesty* (1584), and then in Greek romance and various Italian novelle.[7] All three sources taught Greene the art of leading up to an elaborate and often violent confrontation between the figures of authority and their victims. One of his stories ends with the murder of a father by his long-suffering daughter, another with an armed combat between father and son, still a third with a fight between father, grandfather, and son. *Pandosto* and *Menaphon* each lead to the attempted rape of a daughter by her father, while the second story of the *Planetomachia* ends with a father executing his son for sleeping with his stepmother, whom the father had married in opposition to the son's sage advice.

What place can there be in this topsy-turvy world for the gravely moral story of the prodigal son? Greene reverses most of its assumptions. Precept is of no relevance to experience. Action results from either passion or fortune, forces over which the individual exercises no moral control. Woman is exalted and her chief virtue, stoic resignation, which is the opposite of the active, civic virtue championed by the humanists, celebrated. Nor does Greene maintain the humanists' conservative belief in the wise and benevolent order of society. Parents, who in Greene are most often rulers as well, are unjust, tyrannical, even unnatural. Another of the humanists' prime tenets, that nurture is superior to nature, is ignored. Greene rarely mentions nurture. His characters appear on the scene with no hint as

to how they became what they are. Only *Pandosto* and *Menaphon*
describe the process of growing up, and there Fawnia and
Pleusidippus are unmistakeably royal despite their rustic environment.

At this point one might ask, "Why bother contrasting these
two traditions? Isn't Greene's fiction, with its obvious debts to
Greek romance and the Italian novella, simply irrelevant to the
didactic pattern of prodigality?" Had Greene been content to
leave the two traditions apart, had he been willing not to mix
moral profit with romantic pleasure, there would be little reason
for our doing so. But he was not. Like Lyly, who hung on to the
prodigal son story even in *Euphues and his England*, Greene
found it, if not indispensable, then very nearly so. It embodied a
set of attitudes too prevalent to be dismissed. Greene was, as I
have suggested, freer than Lyly and could on occasion escape,
as he does in *Menaphon* (1589) to an Arcadian world of the pure
aesthetic—an escape sanctioned perhaps by the reputation of
Sidney's *Arcadia*, though probably neither Greene nor his
friends had actually read Sidney's still unpublished romance.[8]
Had they read it, particularly in its first version, they would
have found that not even Sidney could quite avoid the moral
pattern. But unless they hazarded some such flight into the
realm of pure beauty and pure accident, Greene and his
contemporaries were stuck with a reality that included the
paternal warning of moral consequence. The question for them
was not whether to adopt that pattern, but rather, accepting it
as given, how either to get around it or to refute it. Greene tries
one of these strategies in *The Card of Fancy* (1584), the other in
Pandosto (1588).[9]

The Card of Fancy begins with the prodigal son story, though
modified in accordance with Greene's altered sense of things.
The tyrannous Duke Clerophantes of Metelyne has two children, a beautiful and virtuous daughter, Lewcippa, and a son,
Gwydonius, handsome and witty but given over to prodigality.
Clerophantes remonstrates with his son whose impertinent
response echoes Euphues' to Eubulus: "You old men most unjustly, or rather injuriously, measure our stayless mood by your
staid minds" (IV, 17). He announces that he plans to leave the

court and spend his days in travel. His father, unlike the loving and wise elders of the education drama, rejoices at ridding himself of his troublesome son so easily, and heartily recommends travel as the best way of choosing "what course of life is best to take." One can "buy that by experience which otherwise with all the treasure in the world he cannot puchase" (IV, 19), he says, reversing the opinion of Erasmus and Ascham. He does not, however, let his son go without giving him a lengthy dose of sounder paternal advice—the standard counsel of moderation with which we are by now thoroughly familiar—which he caps with the presentation of a ring having as its posy *"praemonitur premunitur,"* forewarned is forearmed. All this Gwydonius disregards. It does not take long for experience to bring him to repentance. He establishes himself in the city of Barutta where the citizens "noted him for a mirror of immoderate life and a very pattern of witless prodigality" (IV, 24). Made suspicious by his extravagant expenditure, they imprison him. Abandoned by all, he quickly comes around. "Alas (quoth he) now have I bought that by hapless experience which, if I had been wise, I might have got by happy counsel" (IV, 25).

Here then, aside from the obvious unworthiness of the hero's father and the lack of any mention of the son's education, is a prodigal son story of the most conventional sort. We are, however, only on page twenty-five of a two hundred page romance. Before being reconciled to his father, Gwydonius must experience adventures of a very different kind, a brief account of which will serve both as a demonstration of the fraudulence of Greene's humanistic pretentions in this book and as an example of his plot making throughout this early phase of his career. Instead of returning home to beg his father's forgiveness, Gwydonius goes to Alexandria where, thinking him a poor gentleman, the good Duke Orlanio takes him into his service. Orlanio has a daughter, Castania, with whom Gwydonius naturally falls in love. After an almost interminable rhetorical courtship, his affection is returned and they secretly swear their devotion to one another. Meanwhile, "Fortune, minding to bewray her mutability, brought it so to pass" that Orlanio neglected to pay the annual tribute owing to the Duke of Metelyne, Gwydonius' father. The bloodthirsty Clerophantes threatens war, so Orlanio's son Thersandro is sent to Metelyne to negotiate a settlement. The only positive result of his embassy is that he meets and falls in love with Gwydonius's sister. All would now be well were Clerophantes not intent on war, but "he, as a man having exiled from his heart both piety and pity, bathed his hands in guiltless blood" (IV, 173). He marches his troops to the gates of Alexandria where, after an indecisive battle, they decide to settle the war by single combat. The fierce Clerophantes choses to defend his own cause. Orlanio, not being a fighting man, proclaims that he will give any champion who fights victoriously for Alexandria his daughter Castania in marriage and the Duchy of Metelyne, including the annual tribute, as her dowry. Gwydonius, who had fled into exile after his identity was revealed by a rejected suitor of Castania, hears this news and returns to seek to win his love by fighting his father. Disguised in the armor of Thersandro, Gwydonius enters the lists incapacitated by the inward struggle between "love and loyalty, nature and necessity" (IV, 190). Finally, after passively fending off his father's thrusts, he is moved by love to make a single blow with which he unhorses his antagonist. He reveals himself, is embraced by the warring dukes, claims Castania as his bride, and returns the Duchy of Metelyne into the hands of his reformed and repentant father.

The prodigal son episode thus introduces an action very unlike it in character. Rather than sending him repentant back to his father, love prepares Gwydonius to work his father's reform. Disorder comes not from the son, but from the father. While the children make love, their fathers make war. And in the end love triumphs bringing reconciliation and peace. But love, unlike moral precept, is not a rational tool. None of the young people uses it to bring about peace. They are used by it. Even Gwydonius, who in the final scene is aware of the whole situation, undertakes to fight his father with no larger aim than that of winning Castania. Like the characters in *Menaphon*, these are figures in a formal pattern worked out by fortune and Greene for our entertainment. Two fathers, dukes of adjoining territories, each with a son and a daughter, the sons and daughters paired in loving couples—the symmetry is too neat for a world controlled by anything but an agency beyond rational comprehension. The action thus belies the promise of the title. Greene's fiction is not a card of fancy, an anatomy of love, but an illustration of love's benevolent power. The threatening terms of the title page, "wherein the folly of those carpet knights is deciphered which, guiding their courses by the compass of Cupid, either dash their ship against most dangerous rocks or else attain the haven with pain and peril," ring hollow. There is nothing behind them. After the introductory episode from the tradition of the prodigal son, Greene neglects his moralizing.

The weakness of the *Card of Fancy* is that the romantic fails to subsume the didactic. The two elements do not come together in any coherent design. The lesson of moderation which Gwydonius presumably learned from his unhappy experience in Barutta is not so much reversed as forgotten. Nor is the conflict of reason and fancy in the second part more than apparent. For Gwydonius the way of love is also the way of prudence, and he knows it. Castania is not only beautiful, but rich and well-born. The bar which separates them, Gwydonius's base estate, is the meretricious instrument of the plot. At any time before the outbreak of hostilities between their fathers, he could reveal his true identity, making him her equal and a prudent match. In Barutta he wasted not his inheritance, but only his spending money. That he, the heir to the Duchy of Metelyne, should despair at great length and with much eloquence that "my ambition [is] above my condition" is nonsense. It takes from the rhetoric any but a pretense of meaning, reducing it to mere ornamentation.

In *Pandosto* Greene does successfully join in a single romantic vision a similar story of quarrelling parents and loving children with material from the didactic tradition. Like the *Card of Fancy*, *Pandosto* consists of two episodes that might have been told as separate stories. But though one is tragic, and the other comic, the two episodes inhabit the same moral universe. In both can be found the typical characteristics of Greene's fiction. A passion beyond the control of reason motivates the action of each part, and time, rather than any human agent, resolves the conflicts.

Each part presents the persecution of innocent and helpless virtue by abusive authority, and in each a patiently suffering woman represents moral excellence. And here Greene allows the prodigal son motif, which he weaves into the second part, no independent admonitory life. It expresses not the usual humanistic morality, but the triumph of love.

Greene achieves his romantic remaking of the prodigal son story, much as Lyly did in *Euphues and his England*, by discovering a rightness in the passionate desires of youth; but his pastoralism better represents the abandonment of identity which inescapably accompanies rebellion than does Lyly's courtliness, and his protagonist is ethically more serious than Philautus. Dorastus does reject his father's advice—in this case that he avoid the folly of youth by marrying a princess of the father's choosing—but he rejects it unwillingly. Neither a hapless dupe, like so many of the prodigals in the education drama, nor an open and insolent rebel, like Euphues, Dorastus finds, despite himself, "that he could not yield to that passion whereto both reason and his father persuaded him" (IV, 273-274). And when he meets and falls in love with the seeming shepherdess, Fawnia, he is no less troubled. "Cursing love that had wrought such a change and blaming the baseness of his mind that would make such a choice," his whole rational and moral being cries out against loving one so far beneath him.

Euphistic fiction is known for its exercises in the rhetoric of the divided mind, but *Pandosto* is almost alone in making the conflict dramatically convincing. Here we don't feel, as we usually do both in Lyly and elsewhere in Greene, that the character merely reads a leaf torn from the author's commonplace book. The minds and affections of the Euphuists were, I think, divided, but none depicted the division as well as Greene. In Dorastus, love opposes not a collection of glib platitudes, but the very structure of his conscious being. Unlike Gwydonius, Dorastus has no reason to suspect the essential prudence of love. He does not know that Fawnia is a princess, nor does she. In giving himself over to fancy, he thus sacrifices his sense of himself, and Greene makes us feel something of the agony of that sacrifice.

Pastoral provided Greene an image of the deprivation of identity. To win Fawnia, Dorastus must abandon the outward signs of his rank and assume the dress of a shepherd. But, unlike the usual prodigal, who changes in appearance, as in mind, without realizing it, Dorastus constantly suffers from the impropriety of his new guise. "Thou keepest a right decorum," he tells himself, "base desires and homely attires. Thy thoughts are fit for none but a shepherd, and thy apparel such as only become a shepherd" (IV, 287). He judges himself just as his father would, for his values and his father's are identical. But the story itself takes a larger and more tolerant view, allowing, and even celebrating, Dorastus' unfilial abnegation of identity.

Refusing to distinguish between culpable lust and innocent love, the more conservative humanists regarded metamorphosis as a Circean retribution that necessarily followed the surrender of one's will to fancy, an inescapable descent toward bestiality. Greene was to adopt a similarly punitive notion in *Alcida* (1589), making it one of the earliest evidences of his attempt to reassert moral respectability. In *Pandosto*, however, and in the other works most directly influenced by the pastoral tradition, he expressed a quite different attitude toward the transforming power of love. Most simply, his idea is that in losing oneself, in giving oneself up to the sway of passion, one finds oneself more fully than ever before. *Ciceronis Amor*, published a year after *Pandosto*, illustrates the conceit most fully.[10] In a valley "most curiously decked with Flora's delicates," a place known to shepherds as "the vale of love," Fabius, the foolish son of a Roman senator, is transformed from his doltish ways by the sight of the heavenly beauty of Terentia. He returns to Rome and devotes himself to learning, soon becoming "expert in all gentle and manlike exercise." Greene explains this sudden alteration:

The high virtues of the heavens infused into this noble breast were imprisoned by the envious wrath of fortune within some narrow corner of his heart, whose bands, went asunder by love, as a lord too mighty for fortune, Cupid, the raiser up of sleepy thoughts, dispersed those

virtues into every part of his mind obscured before with the eclipse of
base thoughts. Let us then think of love as of the most purest passion
that is inserted into the heart of man.

(VII, 188-189)

In *Pandosto* love likewise opposes fortune, which had concealed
Fawnia's royal nature just as it had Fabius' "high virtues," and
love effects Dorastus' passage from filial dependence to auton-
omy in adult society.

Success is not, however, immediate. Symbolic rejection of
identity leads first to the loss of property and freedom, as the
disguised Dorastus is imprisoned by Pandosto. Like all his
prodigal forebears reduced to similar straits, he recalls his
father's advice. "But poor Dorastus lay all this while in close
prison . . . sorrowing sometimes that his fond affection had
procured him this mishap, that by the disobedience of his
parents he had wrought his own despite" (IV, 308-309). Nevertheless, he does not repent. And the story soon rewards his
tenacious rebellion with liberty, a bride, and a kingdom, revealing that the intuition of his love was truer than the prudent
wisdom of his father.

Thus in *Pandosto* Greene rights the argument of comedy set on
its head by the schoolmaster dramatists, though he does it
without abandoning their favorite story. The initial scene of
paternal advice, the rejection of that advice, the surrender to
love, the loss of goods and position, the recollection in suffering
of the father's counsel, all this *Pandosto* shares with the didactic
tradition. But the lesson of *Pandosto* is that the pattern of loss
should be neither avoided nor repented. However painful, it is a
necessary rite of passage, a way from childhood to maturity,
from one stable identity to another. Pandosto, who, unlike
Dorastus, had "resisted in youth," pays the price by yielding in
age to jealousy and incestuous lust, passions of an unconfirmed
self. Though Greene leaves this insight unexplored, and thus
later inaccessible to reason when it might have served to defend
romance, he does seem intuitively aware of passion's place in
the temporal scheme of a man's life. It is in something like this
developmental sense that we can best understand the subtitle of

Pandosto, "the triumph of time." Where the humanists had hoped to annul time, through repentance if necessary, making son's time and father's time the same, Greene allows their essential difference, which is not to say that he entertained an idea of progress, of sons bettering their fathers. Once the pattern of son's time is played out, the son becomes like his father. Youthful rebellion restores a fundamentally stable and unchanging society.

To allow rebellion even so much went against the grain of humanistic admonition. But when Greene wrote *Pandosto* in the mid 1580's, a quarter century of relative social tranquillity had taken some of the edge off those warnings. To Greene and his fellows the world looked considerably less dangerous than it had to their fathers. But with the renewal of military and religious conflict in the last years of the decade, the forces of moral right thinking reasserted themselves and brought Greene to repentance.

The central conflict of *Pandosto,* the conflict between reason and folly, faced Greene as a writer of prose fiction. Was he to write for profit or for pleasure? Dorastus' lament at discovering that he loved a shepherdess must have been the *cri du coeur* of many of Greene's contemporaries who found themselves unable to reconcile their humanistic morality with their desire to read and to write romantic tales which violated that morality in every way. "Thy thoughts cannot be uttered without shame nor thy affections without discredit" is a sentiment that echoed in them as they wrote defensive prefaces to tales they suspected indefensible.

Romance is the subconscious of Renaissance story telling. It was harshly repressed by the mid-century moralists. Ascham attacked both chivalric romance and the newer Italian novella, which first appeared in England in the translations of Painter and Fenton as the *Schoolmaster* was being written. "What toys the daily reading of such a book [as the *Morte Arthur*] may work in the will of a young gentleman or a young maid that liveth wealthily and idly, wise men can judge and honest men do pity.

And yet ten *Morte Darthurs* do not the tenth part so much harm as one of these books made in Italy and translated in England."[11]

But romance could not be eliminated. Romantic tales were told, perhaps with a sense of guilt, but they were told nevertheless. The men who told them were obviously embarrassed. They sought to justify their liberation of those narrative forces which in the less troubled England of Elizabeth's reign could no longer be repressed, but with little success. The only conceptual frame readily available to them, as to Dorastus in his perplexity, was the humanists' own morality which distinguished so sharply between rational virtue and irrational vice. Against such a standard, these stories could only be judged vicious. The natural defense of them, the one adopted by Painter, Gascoigne, and Pettie, was that they might serve as negative examples—as warnings against the vice they portray. Ascham's analysis would have made short work of such an argument. A story, unlike a book of doctrine, acts not on the mind, which might be protected by reason, but directly on the will.

Where will inclineth to goodness the mind is bent to truth; where will is carried from goodness to vanity the mind is soon drawn from truth to false opinion. And so the readiest way to entangle the mind with false doctrine is first to entice the will to wanton living. Therefore, when the busy and open papists abroad could not by their contentious books turn men in England fast enough from truth and right judgment in doctrine, then the subtle and secret papists at home procured bawdy books to be translated out of the Italian tongue, whereby overmany young wills and wits, allured to wantonness, do now boldly condemn all severe books that sound to honesty and godliness.(P. 68)

Other writers, perhaps more honest than those who claimed moral profit for their stories, but no less ill at ease, flaunted the want of didactic use which characterized the tales they told. There is something of this bravado in Painter and Pettie's titles; they proclaim their works palaces of pleasure. The bravado is still more evident in Barnaby Rich's defense of his *Farewell to Military Profession*. "For mine own excuse herein I answer that in the writing of [these stories] I have used the same manner that many of our young gentlemen useth nowadays in the wearing of

their apparel—which is rather to follow a fashion that is new, be
it never so foolish, than to be tied to a more decent custom that
is clean out of use." Rich goes on to satirize foolish fashions in
apparel, obliquely satirizing at the same time his own fashion of
writing. He can ward off criticism only by admitting himself, if
not a villain, at least a fool. What Rich counts on, and what none
of the other writers doubts, is that this sort of story will give
pleasure. [12]

Following fashion, Greene moves from the first of these
positions to the second. He begins by advertising his love
pamphlets as warnings against love. *Mamillia* teaches "how
gentlemen under the perfect substance of pure love are oft
inveigled with the shadow of lewd lust" (II, 3). *Gwydonius* is a
"card of fancy." The *Planetomachia* (1585) discovers "the inward
affections of the mind . . . painting them out in such perfect
colors as youth may perceive what fond fancies their flourishing
years do foster" (V, 3). But with *Perimedes the Blacksmith* (1588)
there is a new note; the profit becomes an adjunct of the
pleasure. *Perimedes* teaches how to pass the time pleasantly
telling stories, "how best to spend the weary winter's nights, or
the longest summer's evenings in honest and delightful recrea-
tion" (VII, 3). *Pandosto* and *Menaphon* are presented as mere
illustrations of the power of time and fortune. A marked
decrease in the amount of moral reflection scattered through the
story accompanies this change in Greene's announced intention. The decrease begins as early as the *Card of Fancy*, continues
in *Perimedes*, and culminates in *Pandosto* and *Menaphon*, where
authorial precept disappears entirely. And along with the wan-
ing of didacticism goes a falling off in the number of typically
Euphuistic figures. In *Gwydonius* Lyly's rhetoric is still the
constant vehicle of meditation and dialogue, but *Pandosto* adopts
it only as an occasional decoration, and *Menaphon* explicitly
announces its demise. As Henry Upchear wrote in praise of
Menaphon,

> *Of all the flowers a Lily once I loved,*
> *Whose laboring beauty branched itself abroad;*
> *But now old age his glory hath removed,*
> *And Greener objects are my eyes' abode.*
>
> (VI, 29)

It was not only Lyly's rhetoric but his kind of fiction, the didactic story in which ideas were more important than action, which had gone out of style.

In 1589, the appearance of Thomas Nashe's *Anatomy of Absurdity*, following on the sobering scare of the Armada, signaled another change in fashion. Nashe's *Anatomy* is first a satire on women and those who praise them, "a brief confutation of the slender imputed praises to feminine perfection." It is next an attack on the authors of romantic fiction. "Are they not ashamed in their prefixed posies to adorn a pretence of profit mixed with pleasure, whenas in their books there is scarce to be found one precept pertaining to virtue, but whole quires fraught with amorous discourses, kindling Venus's flame in Vulcan's forge, carrying Cupid in triumph, alluring even vowed vestals to tread awry, enchanting chaste minds and corrupting the continentest."[13] It is hard not to see Greene in this image of absurdity. He was the self-proclaimed champion of women and the most prolific author of love pamphlets of the decade. That Nashe was no contemptible precisian, but a graduate of Greene's own college, St. John's, Cambridge (which years before had also been Ascham's college), and a fellow university wit in London (Nashe had written a preface to *Menaphon*) only makes it more likely that his satire represented a segment of fashionable opinion which Greene would respect.

Even had Greene been less a slave to fashion, Nashe's criticism is of a sort that he was unprepared to ward off. Though he had been successful, particularly in *Pandosto*, in creating a fiction which might dispute the claims of the moralists, he was not able to conceptualize his defense of love. He came closest to doing so, as we have seen, in the episode of Fabius's transformation by love in *Ciceronis Amor*. The Neoplatonism that there and elsewhere provides an occasional idea was not, however, maintained consistently. Herschel Baker, writing of the use made of Neoplatonic doctrine in the Renaissance, has said that, "as a Neoplatonist, one could revel in the sensuous beauty of the physical world and all the while have as his ultimate goal the beauty and virtue of the spirit.[14] This worked for Greene only so long as he was able to divorce his fiction from the claims of *utile.* Neoplatonism could never compete as a rationally defensible moral system. Nor could it, in fact, have been easily made to fit the reality of Greene's fiction. In some stories, like *Gwydonius* or *Pandosto,* love is successful; but in many others it is unfortunate and even tragic, fully justifying its condemnation. And even those where it succeeds contain counterevidence. Gwydonius is successful in love, but Valericus, Castania's rejected suitor, is not. In *Pandosto* both Dorastus and Pandosto love Fawnia. Both condemn their love and in much the same terms, as opposed to virtue and honor. Yet Dorastus' love is an inspired intuition that leads to a match more ideally suitable than even the wholly reasonable one suggested by his father; Pandosto's love is, on the other hand, a damnably incestuous lust which drags him down to despair and suicide. Is love a blessing or a curse? It can be either and so can be embraced by no rational system of ethics.

Thus, once subjected to criticism, repentance became inevitable for Greene. It began with a wavering repudiation of his defense of women. His *Alcida,* registered December 9, 1588, several months before the publication of the *Anatomy of Absurdity,* exposes the three cardinal vices of women—pride, inconstancy, and prattle—vices which oppose the three virtues illustrated in the earlier *Penelope's Web*—obedience, chastity, and silence.[15] But *Ciceronis Amor* and *Menaphon,* neither of which contain any trace of this fugitive misogynism, quickly succeeded these pallid and unconvincing stories. Greene took a more definite step in his *Orpharion* (registered February 9, 1590).

The title page announces that *Orpharion* contains "the glorious praise of womankind," and so it does. But it also contains a satire on women. The narrator has been travelling from one of Venus' shrines to another seeking a remedy for love. "I heard many counsels and read many precepts but all in vain" (XII, 14). Finally, on the slope of Mt. Erecinus he is granted a dream vision of the mansion of the gods. There the immortals are involved in a dispute over the value of love. To aid them in their determinations they call Orpheus and Arion up from Hades. The two poets disagree. Orpheus attacks love and tells a story intended to prove the distructive pride of women. Arion answers, defending his praise of women with the story of the chaste Argentina. Mercury reasonably suggests that the true nature of woman is a mean between these extremes. The vision has, however, a less ambiguous effect on the narrator. "Calling to mind the occasion of my journey, I found that either I had lost love, or love lost me, for my passions were eased. I left Erecinus and hasted away as fast as I could, glad that one dream had rid me of fancy, which so long had fettered me" (XII, 94). So far as the narrator is concerned, Orpheus' misogynous arguments have carried the day.

From the repudiation of love and women to the repudiation of romantic fiction is a short way. Stories are like women. Each entices by its beauty. An attack on one is likely to be an attack on the other. Thus Ascham assaults both love and Italian books. Both work directly on the will, leading a young man into wanton living. Nashe too associates them. So in Greene, one naturally leads to the other. His *Vision* imitates *Orpharion*. In each the narrator dreams of a debate between two old poets called back from the dead, and in each he repents. The subject of the debate in the *Vision* is not, however, love but fiction, specifically Greene's own fiction. Written in 1590, though not published until after his death in 1592, the *Vision* was prompted by an accusation that Greene had authored the scurrilous *Cobbler of Canterbury*.[16] Troubled that his writings had led men to think him so licentious, he considers the ill effect his love pamphlets may have had on youthful readers. Falling into prayer, he begs forgiveness for his literary prodigality. He recalls Luke XV: "Thou wilt not loose that groat, but findest it with joy; thou weepest in the neck of thy repenting son, and killest the fat calf for his welcome" (XII, 207). He feels the movement of grace and, calmed, falls asleep. In a dream he meets Chaucer and Gower. He mentions that men suspect him of having written the *Cobbler of Canterbury*.

Their allegation is, because it is pleasant, and therefore mine; because it is full of wanton conceits, and therefore mine; in some places, say they, the style bewrays him . . . this, father Chaucer, hath made me enter into consideration of all my former follies and to think how wantonly I

*have spent my youth in penning such fond pamphlets that I am driven
into a dump whether they shall redound to my ensuing credit or my
future infamy, or whether I have done well or ill in setting forth such
amorous trifles.*

(*XII, 213-214*)

Chaucer approves of his work. "Wits are to be praised not for
the gravity of the matter," he says, "but for the ripeness of the
invention. . . . Poets' wits are free and their words ought to be
without check" (XII, 214-215). Pleasure and profit can be combined, he argues, and proves it by abstracting a list of twenty
sententiae against love and women out of Greene's books.
Gower disagrees. "I grant . . . the meaning is good, but the
method is bad. . . . In seeking to suppress fond love, the
sweetness of his discourse allures youth to love. . . . Ovid drew
not so many with his remedy of love from love, as his *Ars
Amandi* bred amorous scholars, nor hath Greene's books
weaned so many from vanity as they have wedded [to] wantonness" (XII, 219). Each poet tells a story, Chaucer a bawdy fabliau
and Gower a moral exemplum. Their stories finished, the wise
King Solomon arrives. He takes Gower's part and urges Greene
to abandon all earthly knowledge "and only give thyself to
theology: be a divine, my son" (XII, 279). Greene awakens
determined to follow the advice of Gower and Solomon. He will
finish only his *Numquam Sera Est* before making his repentance
fully manifest in his *Mourning Garment,* "a weed that I know is
of so plain a cut that it will please the gravest eye and the most
precise ear" (XII, 274).

Gower had allowed that Greene's *Never Too Late* (1590) was at
least better than what he had written before, though even it was
"indifferent Linsey Wolsey to be borne and to be praised and no
more" (XII, 235). Whatever its deviations from strict morality, it
is announced as a proper didactic work, "a powder of experience sent to all youthful gentlemen to root out the infectuous
follies that overreaching conceits foster in the spring time of
their youth" (VIII, 3). Here Greene first renounces the "legend-
ary licence of lying" that Nashe had satirized. *Never Too Late* is
"a true English story," set, however, to hide the identity of a

gentleman still living, in the England of King Palmerin. But the disguise is thin, the gentleman plainly Greene. Feeling the sting of remorse, he begins paying attention to himself. Like him, his Francesco is a poor university man who leaves his wife and travels to the city where he falls victim to the amorous glances of a ruthless courtesan. Three years later, his money gone, she gives him the usual treatment. "Get thee out of my doors, for from henceforth thou shalt never be welcome to Infida" (VIII, 106). The prodigal Francesco thus learns to beware the enticement of beauty, but his full repentance and return are delayed until he can experience something of the life of a poor wit in the metropolis. As a gentleman, he naturally refuses to follow any "mechanical course of life" (VIII, 128), and so is reduced to near starvation when he falls in "amongst a company of players who persuaded him to try his wit in writing of comedies, tragedies, or pastorals" (VIII, 128). The narrator, himself a repentant palmer, takes this as the occasion for a critical digression on stage plays, interesting in that he allows plays only if they satisfy the demands that Nashe made on fiction, only if "lechery, covetousness, pride, self-love, disobedience of parents, and such vices predominant both in age and youth were shot at, not only with examples and instances to feed the eye, but with golden sentences of moral works to please the ear" (VIII, 130).[17] At writing plays, apparently not of this edifying sort, Francesco enjoys great success until one day, overhearing some men discussing the renowned virtue of his wife, he is brought to repentance. His departure from the city is marked by the gift of twelve moral precepts which, if followed earlier, would have kept him from his fall.

In his *Mourning Garment* (1590) Greene comes close to realizing Solomon's injunction to be a divine. "I have," he says, "only with humanity moralized a divine history" (IX, 125). The divine history is the parable of the Prodigal Son. We are reminded that, as far as Greene and his fellow writers strayed from the biblical story, they were aware of it as the ultimate source of their fiction. Here, under the pressure of repentance, Greene restores many of the elements that had long been disregarded. The elder brother, the famine, the feeding of the swine, the killing of the fatted calf, all are put back in place. Nor does Greene neglect the later additions of the iconographic tradition. As in numerous medieval versions of the parable, the prodigal loses his substance in an inn to three prostitutes, who, when his coin is gone, strip him of his fine clothes and drive him out. The didactic emphasis of the *Mourning Garment* belongs, however, to the humanism of Greene's own century. He moralizes the story, as he says, "with humanity," discovering "the forwardness of youth to ill, their restless appetites to amorous effects, the prejudice of wanton love, the disparagement that grows from prodigal humors, the discredit that ensues by such inordinate desires, and, lastly, the fatal detriment that follows the contempt of grave and advised counsel" (IX, 120).

Repentance for Greene means turning back to the self, a self defined by biblical fable and humanistic morality. It means too repudiating romance with its image of another self and its toleration of women, love, and folly. Metamorphosis is again only destructive. The courtesans in the *Mourning Garment* are Circes; they "turn vain glorious fools into asses, gluttonous fools into swine, pleasant fools into apes, proud fools into peacocks, and, when they have done, with a great whip scourge them out at doors" (IX, 163-164). Any deviation from reason, from the received rules of conservative morality, can lead only to inner and outer loss, a descent into bestiality. So at least Greene would now have us believe.

There is no doubt that the milieu in which these stories exist is thoroughly moralized. The title pages, dedications, addresses to the reader, and authorial intrusions all speak with one voice. But, when we look more closely, we discover a hesitancy in Greene's repentance. Even he confesses that these reformed works are to be classed with his "amorous pamphlets." At the end of *Never Too Late* he writes, "And therefore, as soon as may be, Gentlemen, look for Francesco's further fortunes and after that my *Farewell to Folly*, then adieu to all amorous pamphlets" (VIII, 109). He calls the *Mourning Garment* "the first of my reformed passions" and "the last of my trifling pamphlets" (IX, 222). Again, a year later, he writes in his *Farewell to Folly* (1591) that "it is the last I mean ever to publish of such superficial labors" (IX, 229)—and so it was. But this lingering farewell suggests that, though he might introduce a moral commentary and might reform the story of the prodigal son, his basic romantic conception of fiction resisted change.

In *Orpharion* the love-forsaken narrator responds one-sidedly to the stories he hears. Arion's praise of women might as well have convinced him as Orpheus' blame. And it is rather Orpheus' tale, based on the *Orlando Furioso*, than Arion's which derives from the romance tradition.[18] Arion's tale, as René Pruvost has remarked, "participe à la fois du fabliau et de l'exemplum" (p. 326). The narrator is thus reformed by a romantic, if somewhat misogynous, tale and not by a more obviously didactic one. Something of the same anomaly can be observed in Greene's *Vision*. On close examination the *Vision* appears as much a covert defense of Greene's earlier work as a repentance for it. Chaucer's tale is, the narrator informs us, just the sort of thing found in the much abused *Cobbler of Canterbury*. It is not at all like what Greene wrote. It is a fabliau, Greene's first. Gower's tale is, on the other hand, just what we have come to expect from Greene. It closely resembles his two earlier tales of jealousy, *Pandosto* and *Philomela* not only in its narrative style, but in its presentation of the heroine as inflexibly chaste and loyal despite the insane suspicion of her husband. In preferring Gower over Chaucer, Greene is not so much rejecting the folly of his youth as preferring the kind of story he had always written over the kind to which he was to turn in his cony-catching pamphlets.

The other works of this "repentance group" show much the same inconsistency. The tale of Francesco's prodigality, on which the palmer bases most of his didactic commentary, is only one of four loosely related stories included in *Never Too Late* and its sequel, *Francesco's Fortunes*. The others could hardly be used as evidence for the same moral lesson. There is first the thoroughly romantic story of the love of Francesco and Isabel. When their reasonable and prudent passion is opposed by her tyrannical father, they elope in the dead of night. They are pursued, harassed, and Francesco is imprisoned; but true love finally triumphs. There is also the story of Isabel's heroic defense of her virtue, a word for word retelling of Greene's version of Susanna and the Elders from the *Mirror of Modesty*. There is finally the host's tale which, with its heroine's rejection of all three of her suitors, might be considered misogynous, but the point is never made. It is told solely for pleasure. And even the biblical *Mourning Garment* contains the pastoral tale of Rosamond, the virtuous shepherdess betrayed by a fickle shepherd.

Despite some remarkable surface changes, the romantic current of Greene's fiction flows unchecked, and repentance had always been part of that current, though before it had involved neither Greene nor the writing of fiction. With the exception of Maedyna in Ulysses' tale in the *Censure to Philautus*, Greene's female characters persist in either good or evil. But from the first his men have been subject to repentance. Pharicles in *Mamillia* repents for fear of exposure; Gwydonius in the *Card of Fancy* and Phillippo in *Philomela* repent as the result of a legal judgment of their guilt; Saladyne of Egypt and Calamus of Ithaca in the first and second tales of *Penelope's Web* repent because of a woman's virtue; King Psamnetichus in Saturn's tragedy in the *Planetomachia* and Pandosto repent and commit suicide when they discover the full implications of their lust. In the pattern of Greene's fiction repentance is to time as passion is to fortune. Fortune brings disorder, usually with the aid of passion, and time restores order, usually with the aid of repentance. Tragedy occurs when passion is not converted by repentance (Venus's tragedy in the *Planetomachia*), or when repentance comes too late (*Arbasto*, Saturn's tragedy, *Pandosto*).

Maxims repeated throughout Greene's fiction warn that folly can end only in repentance. "He which is rash without reason seldom or never sleepeth without repentance" (*Card of Fancy*, IV, 77). "Better it is for a time with sorrow to prevent dangers than to buy fading pleasure with repentance" (*Planetomachia*, V, 58). Virtue buys "fame with honor," beauty breeds "a kind of delight but with repentance" (*Penelope's Web*, V, 139). The shepherd Menaphon sang of love,

> Tis not sweet
> That is sweet
> Nowhere but where repentance grows.
>
> (VI, 41)

And in the same work the narrator breaks in to give his opinion that love leaves "behind naught but repentant thoughts of days ill spent for that which profits naught" (VI, 140). This seeming inevitability is abrogated only for the few lucky young lovers whose passion leads to a prudent marriage—Gwydonius and Castania, Dorastus and Fawnia, and a handful of others. In the "repentance group" these exceptions become rare indeed, perhaps the only one being Francesco and Isabel in the first episode of *Never Too Late*—and Francesco's subsequent folly partially blights even their success.

Although repentance may at first seem a meaningful choice in a world where one has little control over one's destiny, there are increasingly prominent hints that it too, like love, jealousy, and the accidents of fortune, may be no more than a figure in the formal pattern that governs a man's life. The narrator of *Orpharion* concludes with the telltale remark, "I was overtaken with repentance" (XII, 94). In the early pages of the book he had reported seeing the temple of love where men entered rejoicing and left repenting. This is no longer a warning; it is a statement of fact, a fact which "overtakes" him at the end of the book. The poem which the palmer leaves with his listeners in *Francesco's Fortunes* suggests the same inevitability. It compares the course of love to the course of the sun passing through the zodiac. Love is a natural cycle, from youth to age, from folly to repentance.

What emerges is a determinist interpretation of prodigality and repentance like that of *Acolastus*, a play intended to illustrate the Lutheran notion of grace. Greene's work lacks this theological base, but in explaining his own repentances Greene does move toward radical Protestantism.[19] His literary repentance was the child of fashion, and his personal repentance the work of God. In both he was merely a passive object. His long persistence in the folly of romantic storytelling he blames on the leniency of his readers. "Because that gentlemen have passed over my works with silence and have rid me without a spur, I have . . . plodded forward and set forth many pamphlets, full of much love and little scholarism" (IX,221). One thinks of Calvin's image of man as a horse ridden by either God or the Devil and powerless to choose which.[20] As for the personal repentance, it came, he tells us, only in his final illness when God got into the saddle. "I was checked by the mighty hand of God, for sickness (the messenger of death) attacked me and told me my time was but short" (XII, 164). The thought that his life has shown no marks of God's predestined favor brings him to the edge of despair. Others "were elected and predestined to be chosen vessels of God's glory, and therefore though they did fall, yet they rose again, and did show it in time with some other fruits of their election" (XII, 169). But then, recalling God's promise of forgiveness to those who repent, he feels the movement of grace within him. "Thus," he concludes, "may you see how God hath secret to himself the times of calling, and when he will have them into his vineyard; some he calls in the morning, some at noon, and some in the evening, and yet hath the last his wages as well as the first, for as his judgments are inscrutable, so are his mercies incomprehensible" (XII, 180).

The inscrutable and incomprehensible world of this Calvinist God differs little from the world of Greene's romantic fiction with its accidents of fortune and its sudden reversals. In neither, strictly conceived, can precept have any force because the individual has no power to choose his destiny. Yet Greene continues to hope that the example of folly punished with guilt and repentance will keep others from following the like course. He admits that "it is bootless for me to make any long discourse to such as are graceless as I have been" and that "to such as God hath in his secret council elected, few words will suffice," but, he continues, "let my repentant end be a general example to all the youth in England to obey their parents, to fly whoredom, drunkenness, swearing, blasphemy, contempt of the Word, and such grievous and gross sins" (XII, 179–180).

From our point of view, particularly given our acquaintance with a number of Greene's contemporaries, the paradox of an attachment to two seemingly irreconcilable views, the romantic and finally Calvinist view of an inscrutable world governed by forces unknowable to man and the humanistic view of a rational world in which man might govern himself by precept and example, is too easily resolved. Precept has bred its own necessity. What began as a warning of the folly of youth and the need for repentance soon becomes a description of the inevitable course of human existence. Repentance is the acceptance of this inevitability in one's own life. For nearly a decade Greene's heroes had heard the voice of their conscience warning that folly leads to repentance. For some it did. But for others, most notably Dorastus in *Pandosto*, apparent folly was revealed as a higher wisdom. The moral pattern was, however, too strong to be long resisted. At the first touch of the spur, Greene repented his literary folly and retold the prodigal's story in accordance with the pattern of defeat. In the *Groatsworth of Wit* he breaks off the tale of the prodigal Roberto to confess that it mirrors his own life.[21] And in the *Repentance* he tells his life as a prodigal son story, from his disregard of his parents' "wholesome advertisements," through the excesses of his life in London, to his final, inevitable repentance.

The works that followed Greene's literary repentance were also part of the pattern. From prodigality, through repentance, to the service of mankind. Like Euphues, Greene becomes a satiric Eubulus. In his cony-catching pamphlets, his *Quip for an Upstart Courtier*, and his *Groatsworth of Wit*, he exposes the follies and vices which he came to know as a prodigal. Or so he claims. In fact, these works are for the most part catchpenny collections of jest book tales of a very conventional sort. But this only makes it more significant that he should have chosen to subsume them under the pattern of repentant prodigality. It was the one model which all experience, however varied, must eventually be made to fit.

6
Lodge

Diogenes, the satiric moralist in Thomas Lodge's *Catharos*, suggests as the first in a list of remedies for love that "we ought to call to mind that sensuality and lust destroyeth and dissipateth a man's goods in such sort as it handled the prodigal child, who consumed all his substance with harlots."[1] The allusion cannot be taken as evidence of Lodge's interest in the prodigal son. He borrowed it and the thirty pages surrounding it from an early sixteenth-century French book, *La Somme des Pechez et le Remède d'iceux* of Jean Benedicti. But both the source and the sentiment do seem to put Lodge on the side of the moralists. He did, after all, sign his name to this antiromantic interpretation of prodigality. Was Lodge then a less rebellious writer than his friend Greene? The remarks of a contemporary, a certain T.B., would hardly make one think so. Citing *Catharos*, he attacks Lodge for "boldness," "venomous invention," "impiety," and "atheism."[2] Despite its exemplary morality, *Catharos*—like Lodge's career as a whole—reveals in a new guise the familiar tensions of the prodigal generation.

The book begins with a bitter satire of Lord Burghley, the most powerful representative of the generation whose views Lodge now embraces, and it ends by advising the same Lord Burghley to "entertain learned writers about thee" and to "forget not those who deserve with the pike" (II, 63).[3] Literature and soldiering were Lodge's professions, in neither of which he had prospered. But what an odd proceeding—to begin a plea for patronage by satirizing the intended patron! What could Lodge possibly have had in mind? Was he aiming merely at a *succès du scandal*? Or had he some real hope that Burghley would be won over by this preposterous rhetorical strategy? Either way, his book shows the mixture of rebellion and submissiveness, so inimical to a stable identity, which he and his contemporaries seemed unable to avoid.

C.J. Sisson has defined Lodge's as "the life of an incurably as-
sertive individualist vindicating self-will and private opinion
against all the forces of environment."⁴ The same might be said
of Gascoigne, Lyly, Greene, Raleigh, Peele, Marlowe, and many
other young men of their age. Yet it is only a half-truth, for, as
we have seen, these men internalized "the forces of environment" and were thus locked in an unending battle against
themselves. This is particularly true of Lodge, who, as the son of
a Lord Mayor of London and the product of the Merchant
Taylor's School, Oxford, and Lincoln's Inn, bore as heavy a
burden of expectation as any of his fellow writers. Caught
between this expectation and his own desire, Lodge swung
compulsively back and forth, from pleasure to profit, from
deliberate outrage to careful conciliation, from self-proclamation
to self-abasement, never quite able to find a role that would
satisfy both himself and the world. Like Greene's or Gascoigne's, his career demonstrates both the creative and the
self-destructive consequences of such tension. Lodge wrote
much, but gained little. He invented the English epyllion and
the formal verse satire, wrote the first English defense of poetry,
and published the first pastoral romance, yet he was publicly
humiliated by Gosson, imprisoned under order of the Privy
Council, fleeced by usurers, and disinherited. The open Catholicism of his last years only made permanent a posture of
vulnerable opposition that had been his all along. In his self-
imposed ostracism, he resembles both Euphues (whom he made
author of *Rosalind*) and Diogenes. Figures of this sort occur
repeatedly in his work: Oseas in *A Looking Glass for London and
England*, the speaker in *Scilla's Metamorphosis*, Robert in *Robert,
Duke of Normandy*, Philamis and Celio in *Euphues' Shadow*, Saint
Anthony in *The Devil Conjured*, and Arsinous in *Margarite of
America*. Defeated and disappointed, like Lodge himself, these
characters, though superior in wit or virtue or faith, are yet kept
by that very superiority from occupying an ordinary, respectable, and rewarding place in society. For the former rebel, there
can be no reintegration. Prodagality and romance may be follies
of youth, but the antagonism they express toward the settled
mores of society persists despite youth's passing.

My inclination is to say that Lodge could imagine himself only in the roles of defiant prodigal or isolated critic, never in that of simple participant. But that inclination is checked by Lodge's own reticence. Unlike Gascoigne, Lyly, Greene, or Sidney, Lodge rarely invites his reader to make the leap from literature to life. Prodigal and critic may be the roles most often dramatized in his fiction, but Lodge does not ask us to think him the one playing those roles. On the contrary, he deliberately removes himself from his work. Except in the *Alarm against Usurers*, which does suggest a likeness between author and protagonist, Lodge enjoyed pretending that he was no more than a presenter or translator of other men's work. *Rosalind* he humorously attributes to Euphues and *Euphues' Shadow* to Philautus; he drew *Robert of Normandy* "out of the old and ancient antiquaries" and claims to have found his *Margarite* in a Spanish Jesuit library in America; and, like Pettie, Gascoigne, Sidney, and even Euphues, who Englished Plutarch's *Of Education* and Ovid's *Remedy for Love*, he accomplished the final act of literary self-abnegation by becoming a true translator. But even in his career of romancer, Lodge avoided the usual hints of an autobiographical dark conceit, confining his presence to dedications and prefaces. Thus the similarities we discover between Lodge and his characters must be approached with particular caution. They figure as part of an historical and biographical response to his work, but they do not have the same obvious place in a strictly literary response—not, that is, if such a response hopes to respect the author's intention. Despite the notorious difficulty of determining an author's intention, it does now seem clear, as many recent critics and philosophers have argued, that we can hardly make sense of any utterance, whether written or spoken, without making some inference about the purpose that informed it.[5] And in the case of Lodge (with the notable exception of his *Alarm*), the informing purpose seems not to have included any desire that his biographical face be seen behind the fictive mask of his creation. If I transgress that desire so far as to point out that his later work foreshadows the shape of his life, it is with the understanding that in doing so I leave literary criticism for biography.

The exception to the rule of Lodge's autobiographical reticence is, as I have said, *An Alarm against Usurers,* his first published work. "Truly, gentlemen," he there asserts, "this that I write is true. I myself know the paymaster" (I, 18). And not only the dealings with usurers resemble what those "courteous friends, the gentlemen of the inns of court," to whom he addressed the *Alarm,* would surely have known about the life of their fellow student. Like Lodge, his protagonist is a university man with a considerable inheritance, who is connected with the inns of court, whose loving mother has died, whose father's patience wears thin, and who serves a term in prison. But there are differences too, and these must have been just as important to Lodge's rhetorical purposes as the similarities. By writing the work and thus exposing the practices of usurers, Lodge proclaims his own reformation: his mastery of precept and his application of it in his own life. The protagonist of the *Alarm* goes the other way; he does not repent but rather gives himself over to the unsavory work of the usurer who undid him. Where Lodge writes to warn against prodigality, the hero of his story becomes a maker of prodigals. In 1583 Lodge may have felt it necessary to assert both these possibilities; he needed both to show that he had learned his lesson and was capable of reform and to warn of the extremity to which despair might lead him were help not forthcoming. He needed to do these things, because his young life had reached a point of crisis. His first book, a defense of poetry against the attacks of Stephen Gosson, had been refused a license and had never been distributed. Its author was "hunted by the heavy hand of God" (or so it seemed to Gosson) and proclaimed "little better than a vagrant, looser than liberty, lighter than vanity itself."[6] In the preface to the *Alarm,* Lodge acknowledges these charges, defending himself against the personal vilification of Gosson's rebuttal, but backing down from his defense of poetry. He admits that his opponent had "a good cause" (I, 7). More, however, than Gosson's attack weighed on Lodge. The three or four years that separate *Honest Excuses* from the *Alarm* also saw his brush with the Privy Council and the exhaustion of the fortune (some £1000 in Sisson's estimation) left him by his mother.[7] And by 1583 his relationship with his father had come to such a dangerous pass that, as his biographers have suggested, his recantation of poetry "ought to have been addressed to Sir Thomas . . . . Both it and the *Alarm* to follow were written with one eye upon him."[8] The *Alarm* was registered with the Stationer's Company on November 4, 1583. A little more than a month later, Sir Thomas drew up his will, omitting all mention of his namesake. In February he died, his will unchanged. If the *Alarm* was intended to mollify Sir Thomas, it failed. And well it might, for its prudent conciliation was coupled with still another act of rebellion; bound up with the *Alarm* was another work of quite opposite nature, the *Delectible History of Forbonius and Prisceria*. The second half of the volume thus undermined the apparent rhetorical intentions of the first, revealing that young Thomas, despite his various misfortunes, had still not learned to leave pleasure alone.

This curious production nicely illustrates the divided consciousness of the 1580's and the use each strain made of the pattern of prodigality. *Forbonius and Prisceria* is a widely unrealistic tale of romantic love, while the *Alarm* is so realistic as to seem hardly a story at all, yet the sequence of admonition and rebellion shaped them equally. Each has a witty and weak willed protagonist, a wise and fatherly counselor, and a plot that leads from folly to imprisonment. But neither ends in quite the usual way. Despite the warnings of age, *Forbonius and Prisceria* grants its lovers a joyful marriage, while the *Alarm*, as we have seen, leaves evil rampant, unreclaimed by repentance. In their attitudes toward love, toward women, toward authority, and toward moral freedom, the *Alarm* and *Forbonius* are radically opposed. One intends profit, the other pleasure. One is addressed to the gentlemen of the inns of court, the other to ladies and gentlewomen. One satisfies reason, the other fancy. Where one combines autobiography, satire, and realism, the other eschews all three, preferring instead a romantic world far removed in time and space from the real world of sixteenth-century London. And though each establishes in a scene of sage counsel the humanistic standard of morality, the *Alarm* strongly affirms it, while *Forbonius and Prisceria* rejects it, though most unconvincingly. Lodge was clearly able neither to integrate his two worlds, nor to choose one over the other. Yet his inclusion of the pattern of prodigality in each suggests that either set of conventions had to be related back to his bedrock experience of the struggle between age and youth for the control of youth's identity. Despite his capitulation to the anti-poetic arguments of Gosson—arguments produced at the behest of the Aldermen of London—the control of Lodge's own identity and the identity of his creative work remained very much in doubt.

Ambivalence continues in *Rosalind*, Lodge's next and most successful fiction. But the ambivalence is, for once, more apparent than real. Though by its fictive authorship *Rosalind* asserts its tie to the traditions of didactic fiction, it obviously belongs rather to romance—a less problematic variety of romance than we have before encountered. The book is Euphues' legacy to the sons of Philautus. They are to "read it . . . to profit by it," the chief profit being the avoidance of love. Yet despite Euphues' intentions, *Rosalind* is likely both to undermine our faith in the efficacy of rhetoric as a tool of moral instruction and to leave us unconvinced that love either can or should be avoided. *Rosalind* is thus Lodge's most thoroughgoing answer to humanistic principle and expectation. And though not intended as a defense of poetry, it does nevertheless create a more persuasive image of the world to which poetry belongs than did Lodge's answer to Gosson. In the forest of Arden, the pastoral *locus amoenus* of *Rosalind*, one can violate the more restrictive paternal warnings yet establish, even while doing so, an identity that need not be repented.

It has sometimes been thought that in this happy story Lodge fashioned an exculpating self-image. Sisson suggested that the sibling rivalry depicted in *Rosalind* is "almost ludicrously parallel" to the conflict between Lodge and his brother William, a conflict that Sisson discovered in Elizabethan legal records. According to Sisson, Saladyne, the elder brother "who defrauds Rosader of his dues, makes havoc of his legacies and lands, and spoils his manor houses," reflects William, while Rosader, the maltreated younger brother, is "an artistic and idealized portrait of Lodge [himself]."[9] Now were this so, and were it part of

Lodge's intention that we recognize it to be so, *Rosalind* would mark a considerable departure from that "paradigmatic" regularity which I defined in the first chapter. Here Lodge would be associating himself not with a defeated prodigal, but with a successful lover. He would, in effect, be saying, that he had disregarded antiromantic precept and prospered. But it is not so. *Rosalind* may run contrary to the moral teachings of mid-century humanism, but not quite so openly as that. It is impossible to say whether Lodge noticed the "ludicrous" parallel between his life and his story, but he surely does not encourage us to look for it. Nor is it so obvious that it would have forced itself on the attentions of a contemporary. On the contrary, it is unlikely that *any* early reader would have recognized the parallel, for the quarrel on which such recognition would have had to be based broke out openly only in 1593, three years *after* the publication of *Rosaline*. Unlike the *Alarm against Usurers*, *Rosalind* presents not the real self in the real world, but rather a romantic others.

Walter Davis has argued that for Lodge in *Rosalind* the romantic other was in fact more real than the supposedly real world of conflict and guilt which it replaces. "His thesis, the possibility he explored, was," in Davis's words, "that the world as we know it, with its selfishness and violence, is only the apparent world, whereas the real world is something we never see, an ideal of humility and love."[10] Much in the book would seem to justify this interpretation. For the harsh revenge which had marked the end of brotherly feuding in his source, the fifteenth-century *Tale of Gamelyn*, Lodge substituted reconciliation. He made the story over in the likeness of a more benign vision of human destiny, introducing a pastoral interlude which works a renewal of concord. And what is more, he departed just as sharply from the prodigal son fiction of his contemporaries. Though the book does begin with the usual scene of paternal admonition, and though its central character does violate that admonition by falling in love, neither he nor anyone else ever notices this violation. The keynote of Rosader's character is, on the contrary, fidelity to the memory of his father. Somehow he escapes all sense of guilt. Only in Greene's *Menaphon*, one of the very few fictions of the 1580's that wholly eschews the pattern of prodigality, can another such untortured protagonist be found. And not even Greene achieves as innocent a wooing and as harmonious a resolution as Lodge does in *Rosalind*. Yet neither prodigality nor guilt are completely absent from *Rosalind*. By a most astute sleight of hand Lodge has rather transferred them from the center to the periphery, from the protagonist to his fraternal rival. The crisis of conscience, the rebellion against paternal precept, the imprisonment and repentance—all these elements of the usual prodigal son story Lodge retained, but attached them to the secondary figure of Saladyne. Unlike Rosader, Saladyne does have to renounce something of his own nature to achieve reconciliation with a world that better fits his father's description of it than his own ambitious expectation.

The inclusion of the paradigm of prodigality, even though Lodge shunts it a bit to the side, must, given the evidence of his other fiction, be termed compulsive. Even in *Rosalind*, he was evidently less sure than Davis would have him of his "Platonic view of reality." The disobedience and guilt of Saladyne are just as real, in Davis's philosophical sense, as Rosader's "love and humility." *Rosalind* is a pastoral romance, and it opposes, as does all pastoral, two worlds—here the court of the usurping king Torismond and the forest of Arden. But these two worlds are not governed, as Davis would have it, by fortune and nature, though these are the governing forces in *As You Like It*, Shakespeare's adaptation of *Rosalind*—an indication of the difference between Shakespeare's sense of reality and that of Lodge or of any other romancer of the 1580's, with the possible exception of Spenser. In *Rosalind* not fortune and nature, but rather fortune and love dominate the two worlds, and love is no more or less natural and thus no more or less "real," than fortune. Both are "maladies," a word that occurs again and again in Rosalind with reference both to love and to the aspiring pride provoked by fortune. Both express man's fallen nature and distort his ideal nature. Sir John, in his legacy of good advice, warns against both. "Climb not, my sons. Aspiring pride is a vapor that ascendeth high, but soon turneth to a smoke . . . But, above all,' and with that he fetched a deep sigh, 'beware of love, for it is far more perilous than pleasant' " (I, 11-12).

Euphues, the book's fictive author, who on his deathbed wrote
Rosalind as a legacy to the sons of Philautus, objects in particular
to love. "They shall find love anatomized by Euphues with as
lively colors as in Apelles' table: roses to whip him when he is
wanton, reasons to withstand him when he is wily" (IV, 6).[11]
But, if neither the pride of the courtly world nor the love of the
pastoral properly expresses a man's better nature, it is also true
that neither can be cured by reason and rational persuasion. In
Rosalind the flowered rhetoric, for which Euphues is famed,
makes nothing happen. The book reveals a disjunction between
reason and action that renders nugatory both Euphues' persuasion and Sir John's. "Persuasions are bootless," the shepherd
Montanus observes, "reason lends no remedy, counsel no
comfort, to such whom fancy hath made resolute" (I, 120). But
reality, as Lodge knew it, does come within the rationalists'
scope. The world is as they describe it, though only after experiencing the madness of love or pride can a rational percep-
tion like theirs be achieved. So it was for Euphues, and so, if we
may judge by his sigh, it must have been for Sir John.

The pain of either love or aspiring pride can be cured only by
possession of the thing desired. Saladyne, his "heart fired with
the hope of present preferment," thinks, "Riches, Saladyne, is a
great royalty, and there is no sweeter physic than store" (I, 16),
and the amorous shepherdess Phoebe writes to her beloved
Ganymede, this "malady hath no salve but thy sweet self" (I,
116). The cure for love is apparently effective; we are made to
believe that once united the lovers will live happily ever after.
The cure for the ailment associated with fortune involves greater
danger than the illness, for it makes one liable to the envy of
others. Saladyne no sooner dispossesses his brothers than he is
himself dispossessed and thus reduced to repentance. Love is
cured by marriage, pride by repentance. His pastoral fiction has
allowed Lodge to distinguish, as the mid-century moralists
never did, between two kinds of madness, ambition and love,
and to assign the pattern of prodigality only to the former.

The shepherdess Phoebe fails to make this distinction and
thus provides a test case. She identifies love and fortune and
reacts to the first as one should to the second. "I count it as great

honor," she says, "to triumph over fancy as over fortune" (I, 105). In retribution for her scorn love afflicts her with an "uncouth" passion, a lesbian desire for the disguised Rosalind, a desire which she, in good prodigal fashion, must finally repent. Love is a necessary evil. Even Sir John ruefully admits, "Women are wantons, and yet men cannot want one" (I, 12), and the wise old Coridon, the Eubulus of the woods, agrees. He considers love no better than madness, but realizes that its rejection is still worse—for society, if not for the individual. Commenting on Phoebe's disdain, he says, "But of this I am sure . . . if all maidens were of her mind, the world would grow to a mad pass, for there would be great store of wooing and little wedding" (I, 97). Now this reluctant admission of the irrational hardly amounts to a "Platonic view of reality," but it does relieve youthful fancy of the burden of bad conscience, and that alone, in the context of Elizabethan fiction, is a considerable accomplishment.

The opposition of two worlds gives Lodge a way of avoiding the always embarrassing choice between reason and passion, between morality and love. Just as their pastoral disguises allow his courtly heroes and heroines to act out their amorous impulses without suffering the usual moral inhibitions, so the pastoral form permits the author to write of successful love, without condoning love's folly. In the forest, outside the rigid rational structure of civil life, passion expresses itself with no harm to society. Lodge thus forestalls the stark choices that characterize Greene's fiction even at its most harmonious. In neither *Pandosto* nor *Menaphon* is the pastoral world free of the court; the exigencies of conscience are as pressing, the threat of fortune as great. For Rosalind and Rosader, there is no real doubt, as there is for Dorastus and Fawnia, about the prudence of their love. Only Saladyne, the repentant prodigal, whose humility is being tested, woos without knowing the true rank of his beloved. Lodge's portrayal of authority reveals the same avoidance of the clash of opposing loyalties. In *Rosalind*, as in Greene's fiction, authority is abused—but by usurpers like Saladyne and Torismond, not by a legitimate ruler like Pandosto. Sir John of Bordeaux and the true king Gerismond are benevolent. Lodge thus escapes the dilemma that in Greene is so suggestive of Beaumont and Fletcher, a choice between abusive authority and none at all, between blind obedience and rebellion.

Lodge did not repeat the harmonious resolution of *Rosalind*. His succeeding fictions take place in a bleaker world, a world of sharp, and finally irreconcilable conflict. *Rosalind* marks the end of an epoch for the Elizabethan prodigals, though our familiarity with Shakespeare and the shape of his career may keep us from noticing it. To us the 1590's, the years of *A Midsummer Night's Dream, Romeo and Juliet, Henry IV, Part I*, and *As You Like It*, inevitably seem bright and gay. But to the university educated writers of Lodge's generation, the nineties were anything but gay. For them, repentance was in the air. The second phase of prodigality, the phase of successful rebellion, which had begun ten years earlier with *Euphues and his England*, Greene's *Mamillia*, and Lodge's *Honest Excuses*, reached its summit and its end in 1590, the year that saw the publication of *Rosalind*, the revised portions of Sidney's *Arcadia*, and the first three books of *The Faerie Queene*. But the signs of change were already upon them. Sidney had died four years earlier, Greene was beginning his long repentance, and Lyly his long silence. For whatever reasons—and there are many, including war with Spain, rapid inflation, the Marprelate Controversy, the weariness of a regime that had been too long in power, and the aging of the writers themselves—for whatever reasons, the nineties were hostile to romantic literature. By the middle of the decade, even Spenser, one of the few writers born in the 1550's to escape the opprobrium of prodigality, thought himself hounded by the Blatant Beast of envy and malicious detraction, the worldly enemy of poetry and of any extraordinary accomplishment. His last published work, the final three books of *The Faerie Queene*, portrays the dissolution of Colin Clout's vision and the destruction of his pastoral world. If even Spenser was affected, how could Lodge escape? Of course, he didn't. Though he continued writing romances until 1596, his hold on the spacious sense of human freedom, the harmonious union of reason and desire that animated *Rosalind,* as it had animated *Pandosto, Euphues and his England,* and the middle books of *The Fairie Queene,* failed. Rather than imitating these romantic triumphs, the fiction he wrote after *Rosalind* depicts the inhospitable world of the malcontent nineties. *The Life of Robert, Second Duke of Normandy* (1591), *Euphues' Shadow* (1592), and *A Margarite of America* (1596) lead inexorably to the renunciation of fiction.

Something of Lodge's new skepticism toward poetry and toward beauty more generally is expressed in the last of these fictions by one of the book's wisest and most prudent characters, old Arsinous's daughter Philenia. She clearly feels the need to pass beyond sensual gratification, to allow it only a temporary and narrowly circumscribed place in her life. Her lover, Minecius, woos her with song while disguised in a "pastoral habit." She delights in his verse, as any girl should, but in deciding to accept his love she looks forward to the fading of his courtly wit. "Philenia consented to yield him favor who sought it, knowing that his wit like the rose being more sweet in the bud than in the flower would best fit her, and, as the herb euphemerus that hath in his spring a sweet and purple flower, but being of ten days growth conceiveth nothing of beauty, but is replenished with barrenness, so course of time would change him, she made choice of him" (III, 16). The terms of this reflection are most curious. She anticipates the gradual decline in marriage of the wit that she so much appreciates in courtship, preferring "barrenness" to sweetness and beauty. Lodge's description of the home in which she has been brought up prepares us to understand her attitude and perhaps his own. In the midst of "this rare fortress," this palace of sensual delight, "situate by a gracious and silver floating river, environed with curious planted trees to minister shade, and sweet-smelling flower to recreate the senses," we find an incongruous poem *Humanae Miseriae discursus,* an anatomy of the ages of man. One of its stanzas summarizes and universalizes the futile experience of the prodigal son.

> *His greatest good is to report the trouble*
> *Which he in prime of youth hath overpassed,*

How for his grains of good he reaped but stubble,
How lost by love, by folly's hue disgraced,
Which whilst he counts his son perhaps attendeth,
And yet his days in self-like follies endeth.

                                                            (III, 10)

Here is perhaps the source of Philenia's wisdom. This early in the story, it seems a bit of gratuitous morbidity, just as her reflection seems a harsh defiance of the reigning spirit of romantic love—but both are justified by the unreasoning evil that, masking as courtly wit, is soon to invade and eventually to destroy their pleasant world.

In *Rosalind*, as in *Gwydonius, Pandosto,* or *Menaphon,* poetry, mimetic play, and a lush pastoral setting contribute to the making of a "second self," a self freed from the retribution threatened by humanistic precept.[12] Neither *Robert of Normandy* nor *Margarite of America* permits such freedom. The poets, pastoral actors, and devotees of pleasure in these works are representatives of evil, the Sultan of Babylon in *Robert of Normandy* and Arsadachus in *Margarite of America.* But the odd thing is that, in a unique departure from the autobiographical reticence that otherwise characterizes these later works, Lodge makes us feel that both the Sultan and Arsadachus stand for him in his role of poet. Their poems, he seems to suggest by virtually ignoring the fictional frame in commenting on them, are his own, and he is quite proud of them. Yet, as he tells us in introducing a selection of ten songs that Arsadachus, dressed as a shepherd, sang to his mistress Diana, they give "certain signs in him of an excellent wit, but matched with exceeding wickedness" (III, 74). Though the modern reader may find neither great wit nor great wickedness in these pallid experiments in versification, Lodge apparently expected us to find both and to recognize that both belong as much to him as to his evil characters. He also expected us to recognize that such evil could not be redeemed by mere repentance. The Sultan and Arsadachus must be violently overthrown—and so, we suppose, must that side of Lodge that identified with them. Those who do the overthrowing, Robert in *Robert of Normandy* and Arsinous in

Margarite of America, are men who have completely severed themselves from the world of sensual beauty.

In these last fictions, Lodge takes up again the battle against prodigality, but with new arms—not with the humanistic morality of the middle way, but with magic and mortification of the flesh. In the process, his work attains a mythic and spiritual dimension lacking in Lyly, in Greene, or in his own earlier stories, a lack that testifies to the effect on these young men of their English, Protestant, and humanistic upbringing. Despite the biblical origin of their source, a parable which on the Continent was inspiring works of fervent piety, the other Euphuists never achieve a more than lukewarm sense of supernatural presence. Euphues does become a recluse, but his only proof of divinity, "Euphues and Atheos," is a dull exercise in spiritual sophistry. His cell on Mt. Silixsedra has the scent of priggishness rather than sanctity. As for Greene, though he was directed by Solomon to "be a divine," religious fervor animates only his deathbed repentance. George Pettie's "Alexius," the last story in the *Petite Palace*, shows what might happen to a saint's life in the hands of one of these English authors. Pettie alludes in a single sentence to the grotesquely baroque story of Saint Alexius's pilgrimage, poverty, and self-mortification, and devotes the remainder of the twenty-three pages "trifle" to the rhetorical elaboration of various set themes. Hagiography yields to courtly wit and secular wisdom.

The last six years of Lodge's literary career took a quite different direction. A list of his sources tells something of the difference. They include Albertanus of Brescia's *Liber Consolationis et Consilii*, Girolamo Garimberto's *Concetti*, Gieronimo Giglio's *Nuova Seconda Selva*, Louis le Roy's *Vicissitude des Choses*, Jean Benedicti's *Somme des Pechez*, Joseph Angles's *Flores Theologicarum Questionum*, Luis de Granada's *Libro de la Oración y Meditación* and *Memorial de la Vida Cristiana*, and a variety of other sententious, moral, and theological works reflecting a medieval and Counter-Reformation sensibility.[13] But what Lodge did with his material, whatever its source, tells still more, particularly when his works are set beside those of his contemporaries. Compare, for example, his *Robert of Normandy* with Greene's

Gwydonius. Each is about the son of a duke, a young man who refuses good counsel, gives himself over to vice, repents, and lives disguised in the court of a neighboring ruler whom he defends in battle and whose daughter he marries. But the similarity ends there. *Robert of Normandy* portrays not the transformation of a prodigal into a respectable ruler, but the transformation of a devil into a saint. Murder, mayhem, and rape, not waste and lechery, are his vices. Born with a full set of teeth, his first memorable deed is to bite off his nurse's nipples. In this savage world, the usual humanistic themes are ludicrously out of place, as we realize when Lodge, in a momentary lapse of attention, lets one slip into Robert's repentance. "My youth [was] misspent and worn by woman's guile," he sings, lamenting "how careless wit was wanton beauty's page" (II, 40). This would fit Gwydonius, but what can Robert be thinking of? Perhaps of the night he broke into a convent, stripped the nuns, dragged the loveliest one into a nearby wood, raped her, and cut off her breasts? It is hardly fair to blame the lady! In *Robert of Normandy*, not "woman's guile" but man's abuse of woman defines prodigality. By associating misogynism with prodigality rather than with virtue, Lodge makes way for a repentant return, not to the admonishing father, but to the maternal demi-deity so mistrusted by Protestant humanists.

In his life Lodge accomplished that return with the publication of his *Prosopopeia, Containing the Tears of the Holy, Blessed, and Sanctified Mary, Mother of God* (1596). It announced both his Catholicism and his abandonment of romantic fiction. The next year found him in Avignon, studying medicine at the university, and in January of 1598, after passing a public examination and swearing obedience to the Pope and acceptance of all doctrines "handed down, defined, and declared by the sacred canons and oecumenical councils, and especially by the holy Council of Trent," he was awarded the doctorate.[14] As he moved toward this assumption of a radically new identity—a new religion, a new profession, even for a while a new country—Lodge magnified and projected onto the screen of his fiction the shadow of his impending crisis. Not that he invited his readers to see him in the role of convert. Unlike Gascoigne's or

Greene's, his was a conversion that could not be advertised lightly. Until it was complete and he was ready to act on it, as he did in 1596, he could hardly tell the world that he was on his way to becoming a Catholic. Rather than opening the door to preferment, as Gascoigne's had done for him, Lodge's repentance could only shut it more firmly. But if his first readers were not intended to find in his fiction a proclamation of incipient Catholicism, we can nevertheless recognize, with the hindsight of history, that the books pointed in the direction that the life was to follow.

The retirement from the world and the study of natural magic of Philamis in *Euphues' Shadow* and Arsinous in *Margarite of America* expresses this tendency, as does Lodge's fascination with other contemplatives, Diogenes in *Catharos* (1592), Saint Anthony in *The Devil Conjured* (1596), or Celio in *Euphues' Shadow*. These works set in opposition a world of flesh and a world of spirit, and they require of their characters a particularly sharp break with the past as they go from one to the other. Consider, for example, Robert of Normandy. The rigor of Robert's atonement matches the violence of his youth. A nearly mortal wound, rather than the usual jailing, brings him to a recognition of his sin and his need of salvation. His first penance, imposed by the holy man who finds and cures him, is to walk barefoot to Rome. On his way, he passes through the "wood of temptation," where he slays a lion, resists the charms of a visionary damsel, and overcomes his fear of "hideous shapes of giants threatening him, monstrous tigers assailing him" (II, 43). The penance enjoined on him by the Pope's confessor is still more austere. For seven years he must wear a fool's motley, remain mute, and eat only food that has been thrown to the dogs. The general pattern of sin and repentance and the specific allusion to certain humanistic themes in the early pages of the book recall the story of the prodigal son, but no previous Euphuistic fiction offers a precedent for Robert's atonement. Think again of Greene's Gwydonius, whose repentance was a purely moral awakening, a recognition of the truth of certain paternal precepts, accompanied by no miracles, no prophecies, no visions, no strange or abnormal acts of contrition. Gwydonius humbled himself in Alexandria by living not as a mute fool, but as a fashionable, though poor, courtier. The kind of amorous discourses that Gwydonius freely indulged in are given to Robert's rival and the enemy of Christendom, the sultan of Babylon.

In rejecting that part of himself represented by the sonnet-writing Sultan, Lodge, like Robert, turned toward Rome. He offers his meditation on the tears of the Virgin, the first labor of his repentance, as an aid in the governing of the senses, "certain windows whereat the waters of temptation do enter" (III, 12). But Lodge did not close those windows. He rather opened them on worthier vistas, vistas he found in Baroque Catholicism and particularly in the cult of the Virgin. Perhaps Ascham was right when he warned that "more papists be made by your merry books of Italy than by your earnest books of Louvain."[15] Catholicism answered just those emotional needs excited by romance, while at the same time its new Counter-Reformation discipline satisfied the puritanical drive instilled by humanistic precept. For Lodge, the way to Rome may well have been the way to a reassembled self, though a self no longer permitted the indulgence of romantic fiction. In "The Epistle to the Readers" of his *Prosopopeia,* he prays "that now, at last, after I have wounded the world with too much surfeit of vanity, I may be by the true Helizeus cleansed from the leprosy of my lewd lines, and, being washed in the Jordan of grace, employ my labor to the comfort of the faithful" (III, 13). This he did in part as a translator of Josephus's *Wars of the Jews,* the prose writings of Seneca, a commentary on *La Semaine* of Du Bartas, and several devotional tracts by the popular Catholic writer, Luis de Granada—all works of undiluted profit. But more important was the exercise of his tardily adopted medical vocation. From *Rosalind* on, metaphors of sensual illness, the sickness of love, become more and more concrete in Lodge's fiction, and his hermit-magicians are called upon more and more often to cure real wounds. Now Lodge himself, "cleansed from the leprosy of his lewd lines," literally devotes his labor to healing the world that his vanity had metaphorically wounded.

Chivalric romance and Catholicism are to Lodge as Greek romance and Calvinism were to Greene, or, for that matter, as courtly fiction and humanistic morality were to Lyly. Each kind of storytelling demanded its own particular form of repentance. But these matching pairs explain only the peculiar and local configuration of a more general pattern of experience which Lodge, Greene, and Lyly share. Each was driven by the expectation of conscience and by the pressure of the world from the prodigality of a literary career to its renunciation. In Lyly the element of conscience seems to have been relatively slight, as was his transgression. In Greene and Lodge the inner and outer were more evenly balanced. A change in fashion and a decline in health set Greene on the way to repentance, but these told him out loud only what the inner voice had long been whispering, that beauty breeds delight but with repentance. His humanistic upbringing had taught him to recognize in a shift of fashion a summoning to judgment. So too it must have been for Lodge when, to the misfortunes of the eighties, the quarrel with Gosson, imprisonment, and the loss of his patrimony, were added new goads to repentance, among them the humiliation of neglect. Nashe mockingly dubbed him "The Prodigal Young Master"; Greene admonished him; T.B. attacked him; and the book buying public ignored him.[16] *Rosalind* went through several editions, but none of his labored efforts in verse did particularly well. *Scilla's Metamorphosis, Phillis,* and *A Fig for Momus* were all stillborn. In the last of these, Lodge warned that continued neglect would make him leave off writing.

> *I'll cease to ravel out my wits in rime,*
> *For such who make so base account of art.*
> *And since by wit there is no means to climb,*
> *I'll hold the plow awhile and ply the cart.*
>
> (III, 27)

Lodge pretends a superiority to the philistine world, but it is a pretense that he could not maintain. The world's opinion was too close to his own to be long resisted.

In a way, Lodge, with his Catholic predilection and his interest in medicine, was the luckiest of the three major Euphuists. He had, at least, someplace to go. And though he could not take romance with him, he could take the sensibility that had inspired it. But if by becoming a Catholic and a physician he managed to put together his divided self, it was only at the price of making himself a pariah, a recusant forbidden by law to participate in the civic life of his country. Thus he once again frustrated the ends of his humanistic education. His fiction, with its prodigals turned hermit, showed the way to this peculiar resolution of the problem of prodigality. In it he explored the repentant part that he was soon to play. I do not suppose he had consciously decided to abandon imaginative literature much before he left for Avignon in the last months of 1596. A man who publishes nine books in five years has surely not given up all hope of making his mark as a writer. But when the decision did come, it must have felt right, for it fit a pattern he had been elaborating for more than a decade.

7
Sidney

The question about Sidney is, "Why is he here at all?" Neither his personal reputation nor the reputation of his works makes him a likely subject for a book about Elizabethan prodigals. To those who knew him he seemed the very opposite of one. As Arthur Golding wrote,

> he died not languishing in idleness, riot, and excess, nor as overcome with nice pleasures, and fond vanities, but of manly wounds received in service of his prince, in defense of persons oppressed, in maintenance of the only true, catholic, and Christian religion, among the noble, valiant, and wise, in the open field, in martial manner, the honorablest death that could be desired and best beseeming a Christian knight, whereby he hath worthily won to himself immortal fame among the godly and left example worthy of imitation to others of his calling.[1]

A man of action, but also a man of quick intelligence: "none," as Nashe said, "more virtuous, witty, or learned."[2] After our consideration of *The Schoolmaster, The Glass of Government,* and *Euphues,* of the careers of Gascoigne, Lyle, Greene, and Lodge, this union of virtue and wit should strike us, as it struck Sidney's contemporaries, as an admirable paradox—the unexpected realization of an Erasmian dream. Somehow Sidney found a way of reconciling those antipodes that resisted the best efforts of the Elizabethan prodigals.[3]

More remarkable still, Sidney's *concordia discors* extended from his life to his art. Listen to what some of his contemporaries said of *Astrophel and Stella* and of the *Arcadia.* Matthew Roydon (1593):

> Above all others, this is he
> Which erst approved in his song,
> That love and honor might agree,
> And that pure love will do no wrong.[4]

Gabriel Harvey (1593): "He that will love, let him learn to love of him that will teach him to live, and furnish him with many pithy and effectual instructions."[5] Francis Davison (1602): "If liking other kinds [of poetry], thou mislike the lyrical because the chiefest subject thereof is love, I reply that love being virtuously intended and worthily placed is the whetstone of wit and spur to all generous actions, and that many excellent spirits with great fame of wit, and no stain of judgment, have written excellently in this kind, and specially the ever praise-worthy Sidney."[6] Like Golding and Nashe, Royden, Harvey, and Davison have in mind the commonplace paradigm of youth, a paradigm in which love and honor, wit and judgment, pleasure and profit inevitably clash. What makes Sidney their model is that he managed to still the clash. His work showed them the way past the moral critics and moral qualms that lay in wait for young gentlemen attracted by poetry.

Not only did Sidney's literary practice accomplish a reconciliation of opposites; his *Apology for Poetry* gave that accomplishment a seemingly indestructible theoretical basis. When contemporaries praised his works, they did so in terms that could have been inspired by his own definition of what poetry should be and do. Here too success was unlikely. Their various repentances marked the failure of other writers of his generation to find an adequate defense of poetry. Lodge quickly backed down from his answer to Gosson (himself a repentant author) and ended his literary career telling stories that reveal the dangers of beauty. Greene repudiated his love pamphlets and turned to satire as an act of contrition. Lyly continued to identify himself with the repentant and antiromantic Euphues despite the tentative vindication of love which he had dared in *Euphues and his England*. And, as we have seen, a similar repudiation of amorous devices appears in the work of many others—Gascoigne, Whetstone, Pettie, Rich, and Saker. Even Harington was brought up short in the midst of his translation of the *Orlando Furioso* by the fear of what his "grave and learned" tutor might say if he could see his pupil at work. Self-consciously adopting the role of prodigal (a role played, we should no longer need to insist, by the youthful heroes of many of their fictions), these writers condemn the unthriftiness of their literary endeavor, their wasteful expenditure of time, education, and native ability on an unworthy and perhaps even immoral activity.

Whatever hints there may be that Sidney suffered a comparable uncertainty, neither his contemporaries nor more recent readers have given them credit. That his work does realize the ideal of literature outlined in the *Apology* is as much an axiom of twentieth- as of sixteenth-century criticism. Like Greville, Harington, and Harvey before them, modern commentators, from Greenlaw and Myrick to Rudenstine, Davis, and Lawry, have looked to the *Apology* for an explanation of the nature of Sidney's success; and they have found what they were looking for, whether a definition of moral allegory, heroic poetry, *energia*, or imitation.[7] But though the moderns have been making connections between theory and practice much as Sidney's contemporaries did, the emphasis has shifted. There is no longer much interest in the effect of poetry. The Elizabethans thought more about the practical than the essential. They asked rather what a poem does than what it is, and if the answer did not square with some conventional notion of morality, the poem was in trouble. The *Arcadia* (in Harvey's view) "would enkindle a noble courage . . . to every excellent purpose," preparing its readers (this from Greville) "to set a good countenance upon all the discountenances of adversity, and a stay upon the exorbitant smilings of chance," and even Sidney's lyrics should teach (according to Roydon) that "it is no sin or blame / To love a man of virtuous name."[8] This last may seem sophistically far-fetched, but occasional facetiousness reveals how universal was the expectation that a poem could be jutified only in terms of use. Whatever else we may find in the *Apology*, this surely is its fundamental tenet. For Sidney, the successful poem must not only be the image of an ideal, it must have the power to reproduce that ideal in the mind and actions of its reader, "not only to make a Cyrus . . . but to bestow a Cyrus upon the world to make many Cyruses."[9] The notion was also fundamental to his practice as a poet. "His end," Greville tells us, "was not writing, even while he wrote, nor his knowledge molded for tables or schools; but both his wit and understanding bent upon his heart to make himself and others, not in words or opinions, but in life and action, good and great."[10]

Today the idea of an art which actively shapes, not only the emotions, but also the actions of its readers, an "architectonical art," in Greville's term, inspires disinterest or scorn. "Publicity," "propaganda," or "pornography," we are likely to call it—"impure persuasion," with much emphasis on the impurity.[11] But, however little we may respect it, Sidney's morally muscular conception of poetry is the one we must keep in mind if we want to know what he thought of his work and how his judgment shaped the work itself. Now this is not what either his contemporaries or ours have wanted to know. In making Sidney the answer to their exculpating dream of a gentleman-poet, his contemporaries necessarily ignored any second thoughts that he may himself have had. They found in him an unquestionable hero who was also a gentleman, a poet, and a defender of poetry. Why look any closer? And modern critics, with little interest in the "architectonical" side of Sidney's theory, have been equally unwilling to consider his work as anything less than a triumphant embodiment of a nobly pure aesthetic—even if Sidney thought otherwise, as, if Greville's report is to be trusted, he surely did—at the end of his life if no earlier.

On his deathbed, Sidney was much troubled by the thought that beauty, and particularly the female beauty imitated in his *Arcadia*, might have a bad effect on the actions of its beholder. "When his body declined, and his piercing inward powers were lifted up to a purer horizon, he then discovered, not only the imperfection, but the vanity of these shadows [i.e., the *Arcadia*], how daintily soever limned, as seeing that even beauty itself, in all earthly complexions, was more apt to allure men to evil than to frame any goodness in them. And from this ground, in that memorable testament of his, he bequeathed no other legacy but the fire to this unpolished embryo."[12] Sidney's own judgment of his work does more than reverse the opinion of his contemporaries; it sustains the most crucial of the objections to poetry.

We might wish to dismiss his rejection of beauty as a conventional last minute lapse into piety, but that won't do. Though

the imminence of death may have removed all trace of equivoca-
tion, what Sidney affirmed here he had never felt safe in
denying. Even in the *Apology*, where he easily found answers to
the other "imputations laid to the poor poets," he was unable to
meet the accusation that poetry "was more apt to allure men to
evil than to frame any good in them." The passage in which he
does what he can to get past it deserves to be quoted in full.

*Their third [objection] is how much it [i.e., poetry] abuseth men's wit,
training it to wanton sinfulness and lustfull love: for indeed that is the
principal, if not the only, abuse I can hear alleged. They say the
Comedies rather teach than reprehend amorous conceits. They say the
Lyric is larded with passionate sonnets, the Elegiac weeps the want of
his mistress, and that even to the Heroical Cupid hath ambitiously
climbed. Alas, Love, I would thou couldst as well defend thyself as thou
canst offend others. I would those on whom thou dost attend could
either put thee away, or yield good reason why they keep thee. But
grant love of beauty to be a beastly fault (although it be very hard, since
only man, and no beast, hath the gift to discern beauty); grant that
lovely name of Love to deserve all hateful reproaches (although even
some of my masters the philosophers spent a good deal of their lamp-oil
in setting forth the excellency of it); grant, I say, whatsoever they will
have granted, that not only love, but lust, but vanity, but (if they list)
scurrility, possesseth many leaves of the poets' books; yet think I, when
this is granted, they will find their sentence may with good manners
put the last words foremost, and not say that Poetry abuseth man's wit,
but that man's wit abuseth Poetry. (Shepherd, p. 125)*

If he grants this, he may as well retire from the field. The day is
lost. What use is a defense that abandons the only ground likely
to be attacked—the only ground, for that matter, that either
Sidney or his contemporaries cared to occupy? With all comic,
lyric, elegiac, and heroic poetry that treats of love gone, what
remains to be saved? Nothing of Sidney's own original composition, not the *Certain Sonnets, Astrophel and Stella*, or the *Arcadia*.
Though later poets would pretend that Sidney had proved "that
love and honor might agree," the proof is not to be found here.
As a defense of the poetry that was actually being written in the
last decades of the sixteenth century, Sidney's *Apology* fails. He

surrenders unwillingly, it is true, firing a shot or two in retreat, and wittily claiming victory once safely away from the action. But the shots are poorly aimed and the victory hollow. Take, for example, his parenthetical allegation that the discernment of beauty marks man's superiority over the beasts. It recurs twice in the *Arcadia*. In Book One Musidorus, who was recently "high in pulpit against lovers," reverses himself and falls back on it to defend his love at first sight of Pamela. And in Book Three the same idea figures in Cecropia's temptation of Pamela.[13] In the first instance it supports folly; in the second, evil. In both it appears on behalf of self-interest and in opposition to reason and virtue—a fact which might remind us that, by Sidney's own admission, the *Apology* is another case of special pleading. From Pugliano's praise of horsemanship, he learned, as he tells us in the *exordium*, "that self-love is better than any gilding to make that seem gorgeous wherein ourselves are parties. Wherein," he continues, "if Pugliano's strong affection and weak arguments will not satisfy you, I will give you a nearer example of myself, who (I know not by what mischance) in these my not old years and idlest times having slipped into the title of a poet, am provoked to say something to you in the defence of that my unelected vocation" (Shepherd, p. 95).[14] Youth and idleness are the usual provocations to love. Self-love (*philautia*) is the characteristic fault of the prodigal.[15] Lover, poet, and prodigal, Sidney is less an exception than his admirers would have him appear.

Why a chapter on Sidney in a book about Elizabethan prodigals? Because, from his point of view, he was one of them. Though he does not deserve to be bracketed with the likes of Lyly, Lodge, and Greene, Sidney could not help finding himself "sick among the rest." He suffered the usual ailment of strong affection and weak arguments. His feelings were on one side; his judgment on the other. For all the elegant and courtly irony with which it is expressed, there is real pathos in his wish that those on whom love attends could either put it away or yield good reason why they keep it. We may, however, no longer be able to feel for Sidney's dilemma. Where on one level of our culture we disdain art that pretends to affect action, on another we look to it for help in maintaining sexual performance. On neither are we likely to take seriously the humanists' objection to poetry. In the mid-1970's, half-way to that brave new world where erotic stimulation will be the prime justification of art, it is difficult to imagine that Sidney may genuinely have feared the truth of what a recent film advertisement so eagerly proclaims: "All art is sex!" The beauty of a poem, the Elizabethans agreed, resembled the beauty of a woman. The energy it released was libidinal. But the erotic fire could be justified only if it burned in the cause of civic virtue. Mid-century humanism, the humanism of Ascham, Burghley, and their generation, taught the danger of igniting the sexual impulse whatever the declared aim. Sidney's discomfort shows that, though he rebelled against these arguments, he was unable to disprove them.

He was equally unable to avoid the paradigm of prodigality. His works, like those of the Euphuists and the schoolmaster-dramatists who preceded them, typically begin with a scene of rational and antiromantic good counsel against which the way-ward behavior of his young heroes is measured. But I suspect that Sidney stood in a slightly different relation to this pattern than did his contemporaries. For them its appeal was primarily public. It was a fashionable literary type and might be expected to enhance the success of works intended for publication and sale; at the same time it provided the author a convenient persona, one capable of attracting both admiration for wit and patronage for wisdom. Many of these writers seem genuinely to have felt that the paradigm of prodigality fit their lives, but its evident utility no doubt skewed their response. With Sidney we haven't the same doubts. He wrote, initially at least, for a much smaller and more intimate audience. Publication and financial profit were not among his concerns. Nor, I think, did he expect the image of himself projected in his work to advance his political career. A reputation for wit might have been useful to him at court, but it might easily have been secured with far less labor. His motives, particularly in the Old *Arcadia* and also, though to a lesser degree, in *Astrophel and Stella*, were rather private and experimental. More than any of his contemporaries, he was engaged as a writer in a testing of himself and of literature. The plot structure that Lyly borrowed from the moralists to prove his respectability, and that Greene and Lodge used because Lyly had, was for Sidney a natural expression of his own experience. His life generated the form of his work. I cannot, of course, be sure that Sidney's adoption of this pattern owes nothing to morality plays or to *The Anatomy of Wit*, the only Euphuistic fiction available when he wrote the first *Arcadia*; but although he displays his debt to Heliodorus, Sannazaro, and Montemayor, he builds no apparent bridge from his works to those in the prodigal son tradition. From de Volder and Macropedius to Gascoigne, from Gascoigne and Ascham to Lyly, from Lyly to Lodge and Greene, the line of descent is clear. No such line leads from any of them to Sidney. He seems to have had little interest in the education-drama; Euphuism he disliked; and his only reference to the parable of the Prodigal Son shows him unconscious of the admonitory meaning it had acquired (see Shepherd, p. 109). He does, however, allude often and pointedly to his own life. His upbringing, expectations, and experiences figure largely in the adventures of Pyrocles, Musidorus, and Astrophel. This is not to make of these characters mere allegorical masks for the author, or to make of the works no more than *romans à clef*, though to an extent that is precisely what they were intended to be. They are, however, *romans à clef* of a rather special sort, figuring more prominently the moral issues of Sidney's life than its outward events. Not all the episodes in *Astrophel* and perhaps very few in the *Arcadia* have a direct autobiographical source, but the shape of the works derives from that of the life, and the questions raised by the life become those of the works.

Both the particular strengths and the particular limitations that characterize Sidney as a poet are, in part at least, the result of this autobiographical inwardness. Most of his writings—not only the Old and New *Arcadia*, *Astrophel and Stella*, and the *Defense of Poesy*, but also the *Certain Sonnets*, the *Lady of May*, many of the separate eclogues in the *Arcadia*, and even the tournament of the Four Foster Children of Desire, which he seems to have had a major part in composing—revolve around a very few abstract notions and their interrelation: Reason and Well-Doing, Beauty, Virtue, and Desire. It is with good cause that a recent critic has accused him of lacking a "capacious soul."[16] Though he worked in many genres, his subjects are few and his range of sympathy narrow. If we were to divide the great English writers into two Keatsian categories, on the one hand those possessed of "negative capability," and on the other those dominated by the "egotistical sublime," Sidney would belong to the latter. Birth and education, enforced by a natural seriousness of temper, kept him on a particularly short rein. He could not, as unvalued persons did, carve for himself, for on his choice depended the reputation of one of the most illustrious English families. As he said in his defense of the Earl of Leicester, "My chiefest honor is to be a Dudley."[17] It was an honor—and a responsibility—which determined virtually every word he wrote. Yet strength grew of this restraint. "Man," one of his poems says, "hath strongest soul when most his reins do bow." Though Sidney's character, expectations, and experience marked the limits of his imagination, they also lent an extraordinary moral and artistic force to the work he did within those limits.

If we wish to find Sidney portrayed in his work, the obvious place to look is the Old *Arcadia*. No one doubts that Philisides—a youth in love, a rebel against the counsels of age, a man transformed by passion from gentleman to shepherd, in short, a prodigal, though an unrepentant one—is Sidney's "poetic persona."[18] Whatever the truth of his affections may have been, Sidney, like many of his contemporaries, chose to present himself in the guise of romantic rebellion. In the first eclogues Philisides argues with Geron, the representative of age, taking the part of passion against reason; in the second he disputes with an antiromantic echo, which repeatedly discovers the foolish implications of his plaints; in the third he remembers that his old master Languet hated "what is naught"; and in the fourth he describes his education and tells how love diverted him from the achievement which education promised. In each he presents a division between two opposing sets of values, suggesting that he was brought up with one and now embraces the other. And since this division is also the central moral division of the book as a whole, Sidney's introduction of himself in the eclogues may be construed as an invitation to suppose that the Old *Arcadia* was meant, in part at least, as a work of self-reflection and self-projection.

In 1593 Gabriel Harvey wrote of "the two brave knights, Musidorus and Pyrocles, combined in one excellent knight, Sir Philip Sidney."[19] Without leaping directly to Harvey's conclusion, we do nevertheless arrive at a similar end by the more roundabout means of comparing Philisides with the two principal heroes of Sidney's romance. Like Pyrocles and Musidorus, Philisides has been drawn by the lure of beauty from the life of "well-doing" to which he was born. The very words in which he describes his transformation, "much in state, but more in mind," echo Pyrocles' "Transformed in show, but more transformed in mind" (Robertson, pp. 28 and 335), as the advice which he refuses in the first eclogue resembles that which Pyrocles refused in the immediately preceding Book One.[20] And Pyrocles, when confronted with the naked beauty of his beloved Philoclea, can think of no more fitting blazon than the one which Philisides had composed in honor of his mistress. Playful hints of this sort are just what one expects of literature written for a semiprivate coterie. We have noticed a similar byplay of intimation and innuendo in Gascoigne and again in Lyly. But Sidney's audience was still more limited than theirs and could be engaged with more subtle clues. The first *Arcadia* was written, Sidney tells his sister in the prefatory letter, "only for you, only to you" (Robertson, p. 3). If we extend that "you," as Sidney evidently expected it to be extended, to include the Countess of Pembroke's friends, then I see no reason to doubt Sidney's word. He wrote, initially at least, for readers with whom he shared an easy intimacy, readers who knew enough of his situation to catch his hints and appreciate their meaning. To them he could present his book as the product of "a young head not so well stayed as I would it were (and shall be when God will) having many fancies begotten in it, if it had not been some way delivered, would have grown a monster, and more sorry might I be that they came in than that they came out" (Robertson, p. 3). And to them he could confide, albeit by the indirection of rhetorical winks and nods, that the same fancy laden head was to be seen on the shoulders of Philisides, Pyrocles, and Musidorus.

Trying to decipher the mysterious meaning by identifying half-hidden names and events is a natural and expected response to such teasing suggestiveness. In the sixteenth century, it was probably the most common response. Thomas Wilson thought that in Montemayor's *Diana* "under the names and veils of shepherds and their lovers are covertly discoursed many noble actions and affections of the Spanish nation, as is of the English of that admirable and never enough praised book of Sir Phil. Sidney's *Arcadia*."[21] And the conventions of the pastoral, exemplified by Theocritus, Virgil, Sannazaro, and Spenser, no doubt strengthened his supposition in the case of both Montemayor and Sidney. Puttenham, indeed, thought that the pastoral form was founded so as "under the veil of homely persons and in rude speeches to insinuate and glance at greater matters, and such as perchance had not been safe to have been disclosed in any other sort."[22] Philisides' "Ister Bank," with its allegorical reference to Elizabeth's French marriage, repeating objections that Sidney had stated more openly in his *Discourse to the Queen*, provides an obvious instance of such glancing at greater matters. But not much of the topical allusion in the *Arcadia* is this specific. It may be, as many of Sidney's contemporaries thought and as more recent commentators have occasionally tried to prove,[23] that Philisides' passion for Mira and Pyrocles' for Philoclea expressed some courtly amour of Sidney's own—a speculation encouraged by the narrator's plaint, "But alas, sweet Philoclea, how hath my pen forgotten thee, since to thy memory principally all this long matter is intended," and by his admission of a fellow feeling for the sufferings of Pyrocles ("I myself feel such compassion of his passion"). But even if true, this particular meaning must always have been secondary to a more general concern on Sidney's part with the conflict in his own experience between introspective, literary retirement and the active life of political well-doing.

Nearly fifty years ago, Mario Praz noticed that "in the persons of Pyrocles defending solitariness . . . and Musidorus urging him, instead, to follow that knowledge in which consists the bettering of the mind, and to go back to the service of his own country, we at once recognize Sidney himself seeking for peace at Wilton, after the turmoil of the Court, and his friend and adviser Languet reminding him how his duty should have kept him in public life."[24] More recently, Neil Rudenstine has explored in considerable detail the thematic and tonal similarities between the Sidney-Languet correspondence and the Old *Arcadia*, pointing out that "the debate with Languet on the question of pastoral retirement occupied mainly those letters between March 1578 and October 1580, and this—so far as can be determined—was precisely the time when Sidney was composing the original *Arcadia* at Wilton." Rudenstine concludes that "the parallels are close enough to define much more than an accidental or vaguely peripheral relationship between the two."[25] They are, however, neither close nor sustained enough to make the Old *Arcadia* more than an intermittant allegory. What we find is rather a fictional exploration of certain fundamental tensions with just enough personal coloring so that its first audience might easily have recognized the tensions as those generated by Sidney's own life. Nor is this autobiographical element everywhere the same. On a scale of likeness, the narrator stands so near as to be virtually indistinguishable from Sidney, Philisides a bit further away, Pyrocles and, finally, Musidorus still further. But each begins with an education that intends him for public service and each, "overmastered by some thoughts," as Sidney said of the impulse that made him a poet, is distracted from that worthy goal.

I am quite sure that no one had to tell the "fair Ladies" at Wilton that Philip was to be seen in his book. They knew it, and he knew they knew it. Even four centuries later we are caught in this web of understanding. The Old *Arcadia* calls forth and depends on a particularly personal sympathy. In writing to his sister, Sidney defines the partisanship he expects of his reader. "If you keep it to yourself, or to such friends who will weigh errors in the balance of goodwill, I hope, for the father's sake, it will be pardoned, perchance made much of, though in itself it have deformities. For indeed, for severer eyes it is not" (Robertson, p. 3). Pardon the book, he asks, for the sake of its author. As we read on, the narrator seems to be asking us to pardon Pyrocles and Musidorus, Pamela and Philoclea, for his sake and for our own. He freely admits his subjection to passion and invites his readers, Lady Mary and her friends, to admit theirs. "You ladies know best whether sometimes you feel impression of that passion." But the *Arcadia* makes of sympathy a trap. By his confident insinuation that they, knowing at first hand the power of love will understand, and understanding will pity, and pitying will forgive, the narrator manipulates his readers into sharing the guilt and the awareness of guilt that characterizes Pyrocles, Musidorus, and Sidney himself.

The strategy of entrapment can be observed both in the individual episode and in the structure of the work as a whole. Take, for example, the scene of admonition. We cannot complain that Sidney has unfairly skirted the moral issue. On the contrary, virtue has its say more fully and more cogently than in any other prodigal son story, and yet we are brought around to accepting, even welcoming, its overthrow. This is in part the effect of affectionate involvement, but it also results from detachment. In the very act of engaging his reader in what will soon be an unbreakable net of complicity, Sidney lets him feel superior both to "poor Pyrocles" and to the moralistic Musidorus who judges him. Where in Euphuistic fiction the narrator is either a neutral relator of fact or a defender of graybeard morality, Sidney's narrator laughs at both the admonisher and the admonished. Musidorus's startled naiveté and long-winded vehemence contribute as much to his amusement as Pyrocles' folly, and his attitude excuses us from taking their confrontation very seriously. Moreover, in the *Arcadia* the admonisher himself shows us the way to complicity. Eubulus in *The Anatomy of Wit*, the old Rabbi Belessi in Greene's *Mourning Garment*, and Sir John of Bordeaux in *Rosalind* simply state the moral position and then retire from the story, judgment clear and counsel intact. None joins in the plot against well-doing. With Musidorus, affection overcomes reason. He ends by commanding Pyrocles to persist in the way of passion and by offering his assistance. Within ten pages he has seen Pamela and is "wounded with more sudden violence of love than ever Pyrocles was." And what do we think of this turncoat moralist? We share the amused sympathy of the narrator.

The reader's progress in the first three books of the Old *Arcadia* resembles that of Musidorus in this early scene. We begin on the side of civic humanism, pass through a stage of detached tolerance, and end excited by vicarious lust. We recognize the folly of Basilius's retirement and all along judge without hesitation his passion and Gynecia's, yet for every action of theirs that we firmly reject, we allow another quite like it of Pyrocles or Musidorus until principle is irrecoverably lost in a maze of partiality. What with the bear, the lion, and the Phagonian rebels, the transvestism and *déclassement*, the dark cave of self-knowledge and the schemes of desire, we do not lack for warnings, yet not more than once is the reader moved to whisper under his breath, "Stop! You're going too far!" and even that once—when Musidorus is on the point of raping Pamela—prepares the undermurring acceptance of Pyrocles' success. [26] By the time Pyrocles fleshes his will on Philoclea, we are only too ready for the titillation of vicarious pleasure.

But now the trap into which we have so cleverly been drawn snaps shut. After the cozy complicity of Philoclea's bedchamber, the fourth book begins:

The everlasting justice (using ourselves to be the punishers of our faults, and making of our own actions the beginning of our chastisement, that our shame may be the more manifest, and our repentance follow the sooner) took Dametas at this present (by whose folly the others' wisdom might receive the greater overthrow) to be the instrument of revealing the secretest cunning—so evil a ground doth evil stand upon, and so manifest it is that nothing remains strongly but that which hath the good foundation of goodness. (Robertson, p. 365)

The chimera of sensual delight suddenly dissolves and we are left face to face with moral consequence. In rapid succession Duke Basilius dies, Gynecia, Pyrocles, Philoclea, Musidorus, and Pamela are imprisoned, factions arise, and Arcadia careens toward civil war—and all this the result, direct or indirect, of passions that we have silently approved. Here with Pyrocles and Musidorus we experience, or seem on the verge of experiencing, the truth of that precept which the conventional prodigal son story aims to teach—that, in the words of Musidorus, "the highest end [passion] aspires unto [is] a little pleasure, with much pain before, and great repentance after" (Robertson, p. 20). They, and we with them, have laboriously climbed Mount Infatuation only to topple into the Pit of Regret. Or so the sudden shift in the narrator's perspective seems to suggest. But that is not, in fact, what happens. Unlike the usual prodigal, neither Pyrocles nor Musidorus repents. "We have lived, and have lived to be good to ourselves and others. Our souls (which are put into the stirring earth of our bodies) have achieved the causes of their hither coming. They have known, and honored with knowledge, the cause of their creation" (Robertson, p. 371). In the trial they confess to certain technical infractions of Arcadian law but feel themselves justified by the claims of a love which they refuse to renounce. But while they reject the perspective of "Everlasting Justice," Evarchus, the spokesman for justice, rejects their defense. "That sweet and heavenly uniting of the minds, which properly is called love, hath no other knot but virtue; and therefore if it be a right love, it can never slide into any action that is not virtuous" (Robertson, p. 407). Is he right or are they? Is the Old *Arcadia* a vindication of morality or a defense of love? Was our sympathy based on delusive appearance, or were we right in thinking the loving pursuit of beauty an excuse for inconstancy?

I find it impossible to answer these questions. The first words of Book Five suggest, I think, the effect the Old *Arcadia* achieves: "The dangerous division of men's minds." The story sets father against son, the stable ethos of the mid-century humanist against the inchoate longings of the prodigal courtier, judgment against sympathy, so that, though these opposites are irreconcilable, no choice can be made between them. Evarchus is a man of unquestionable probity. No partiality, not even that of a father for his son, can alter his judgment. And from our own acquaintance with the story, we know how accurate that judgment is. Pyrocles and Musidorus are condemned only for what they have in fact done. Yet we are not convinced that they should die. Massed against Evarchus's judgment is every worldly value—beauty, love, valor, family loyalty, even political commodity. The narrator, who now sides quite unreservedly with Evarchus, can accuse, can even convict us of "examining the matter by [our] own passions"; he cannot make us renounce those passions. We rather hold to them more stubbornly than ever. We become part of the fickle mob that the story has taught us to despise. What is more, we know ourselves to be part of it. And we know too that the one ideally good man stands alone against us, though he has far more reason than we to wish the freedom of his son and nephew. We may remember with some surprise how in the opening pages of the book we so confidently distinguished between right and wrong. Of all those involved in the Old *Arcadia*—characters and reader alike—only Evarchus is at the end what he was at the beginning, "the line of his actions straight and always like itself, no worldly thing being able to shake the constancy of it" (Robertson, pp. 357–358).

One thinks of the explanation Philip gave his father to justify a change in political tactics. "So strangely and diversely goes the course of the world by the interchanging humors of those that govern it, that though it be most noble to have always one mind and one constancy, yet can it not be always directed to one point, but must needs sometimes alter his course, according to the force of others' changes drives it" (Feuillerat, III, 122). In a matter indifferent in itself, alteration might be acceptable, but would Sidney as easily justify a fundamental deviation from the course of well-doing, a transmutation of the self no less marked than that of Pyrocles or Musidorus? This is the dilemma so powerfully dramatized in the Old *Arcadia*, the dilemma of Sidney's generation.

Could duty, as the humanist-statesmen understood it, be reconciled with the pursuit of beauty? This, quite simply, is the question posed by Sidney's romance. For the sake of beauty, Pyrocles and Musidorus relent and slake off from "the main career [they] had so notably begun and almost performed." Basilius's retirement (recognized by many readers as an allusion to Elizabeth's overly cautious foreign policy which deprived the young men of Sidney's age of an opportunity to exercise their virtue in the service of the state) may have prompted the adoption of their demeaning disguises, but the responsibility remains theirs. Painfully aware of this responsibility, they speak through much of the book as men unsatisfied with themselves, men false to their highest ideals, yet when the dreadful consequences of their course are revealed, they refuse to repent. They decide, in fact, that they have maintained "one mind and one constancy," though directed to a different point. But their judgment of themselves does not stand unquestioned. The voice of conscience, the father within, is stilled only to be replaced by the real father. Evarchus has been long absent, but on the last day he returns to pronounce his terrible verdict. Had Sidney been thinking of the parable of the Prodigal Son, he could hardly have contrived a conclusion more sharply at variance with it. Instead of the father recognizing his son "when he was yet a great way off," and running to welcome him, Evarchus refuses recognition. "Nay, I cannot in this case acknowledge you for mine; for never I had shepherd to my nephew, nor never had woman to my son. Your vices have degraded you from being princes, and have disannulled your birthright" (Robertson, pp. 411–412).

But again the question arises: Who is right, Evarchus or the unrepentant Pyrocles and Musidorus? The trial ends in a standoff, with our minds and our affections hopelessly divided. From this dilemma Sidney offers no credible escape. The resurrection of Basilius brings the story to a happy conclusion but leaves the real question unanswered. Its suggestion of a merciful providence can hardly drown out the insistent claims of "the never changing Justice." And regardless of whether Justice or Mercy prevails, the Old *Arcadia* portrays man able neither surely to know nor freely to choose the Good. In Pyrocles' view, not his own will but the "unsearchable wisdoms" of the gods overthrew his desire to serve his father (Robertson, p. 413), and the fifth book resounds with similar doubts concerning human reason.

I am a man; that is to say, a creature whose reason is often darkened with error . . . . [Reason is] many times rebelliously resisted, always with this prison darkened. . . . O corrupted reason of mankind. . . .

So uncertain are mortal judgments, the same person most infamous and most famous, and neither justly. . . . In such shadow or rather pit of darkness the wormish mankind lives that neither they know how to foresee nor what to fear, and are but like tennis balls tossed by the racket of the higher powers. (Robertson, pp. 365, 373, 385–386, 389, 416)

Here we find not only the theme but the experience of the Old *Arcadia*. The great accomplishment of Sidney's book is to make us know from the division it creates in our own minds the agony and perhaps the impossibility of rational choice. It is an experience that puts us in close rapport with Sidney and the other prodigals of his generation.

More surely than either Pyrocles or Musidorus, Astrophel is a mask for Sidney—a braver, bolder, more seductive self, a self new made (perhaps by love) for the purpose of persuasion. One does not so easily pick truth from fiction in *Astrophel and Stella* as to put a biographer at his ease, but this much is clear: the poems invite us to see Sidney in Astrophel and they suggest that his purpose in writing was the simple, if ignoble, desire to seduce Lady Rich. Though replete with shifting roles and changing attitudes, the series constantly supposes an historical occasion. "There is," as Richard Lanham has argued, "no Astrophil in the poem except as a name. It is Sidney who speaks, when he speaks in the 'biographical' sonnets. . . . When he postures, it is Sidney who postures and not Astrophil."[27] Which is not necessarily to say (though it does seem to be what Lanham wishes to say) that Astrophel, any more than Philisides, Pyrocles, or Musidorus, is all there was to Sidney, or that in his own person Sidney would have acted just as Astrophel does. He had other roles and other attitudes more in keeping with the demands of his parents, his teachers, and his own humanistic conscience. Because of his divided heritage, he was to an extraordinary degree capable of putting himself in perspective—of dramatizing and exaggerating one part of himself and judging that part from the viewpoint of the other. But though he was both passionate actor and rational judge, he explicitly identified himself in his fiction and poetry only with the former. He was Philisides not Geron, Pyrocles not Evarchus, Astrophel not Reason. We suppose that the historical Philip Sidney must have had something of the old men in him, because of what we know from other sources and because his books come so near endorsing the position of age. But we see him as rebellious youth for the much simpler reason that he tells us to.

Surely it is difficult even now, and must have been impossible for his first readers, not to recognize in Astrophel's depiction of himself the familiar features of Sidney. Consider, for example, the twenty-first sonnet. Its "young mind," "writings," "vain thoughts," debt of "nobler desires," "birth," "great expectation," "promise," and "decline" are all Sidney's, and would easily have been recognized as his. Or take sonnet eighteen, which again shows the unmistakable Sidnean figure in the typical Sidnean predicament, again with literary waste added to the rest.

> With what sharp checks I in myself am shent,
> When into Reason's audit I do go,
> And by just counts myself a bankrupt know
> Of all those goods, which heaven to me hath lent,
> Unable quite to pay even Nature's rent,
> Which unto it by birthright I do owe;
> And which is worse no good excuse can show,
> But that my wealth I have most idly spent.
> My youth doth waste, my knowledge brings forth toys,
> My wit doth strive those passions to defend,
> Which for reward spoil it with vain annoys.
> I see my course to lose myself doth bend,
> I see and yet no greater sorrow take,
> Then that I lose no more for Stella's sake.[28]

"The Lover as Prodigal" might be the title of this poem, or "The Poet as Prodigal," for those "toys" are (like the "toyful book" of the letter to Robert Sidney) his poems. The sonnet makes sense only if we admit that reason (not our reason, but the conventional reason of Sidney's age) would indeed count as wasted knowledge spent in the writing of poems. And, if we admit this, we are obliged to admit too that reason's judgment of Astrophel is reason's judgment of Sidney, who, like his protagonist, was both lover and poet. We may even recognize in the tenth line ("My wit doth strive those passions to defend") an allusion to the Old *Arcadia* or the *Defense of Poesy*, while the twelfth ("I see my course to lose myself doth bend") may bring to mind Languet's warning, "if only you are true to yourself, and do not permit yourself to be transformed into another person." By any criterion that Languet might have applied, Sidney had been transformed. In the poet and defender of poetry, Languet would hardly have recognized the young man whose noble "condition of life" prohibited even moderate "literary leisure."[29]

Transformation, the violent casting off of the conventional self, is at once the technique and the subject of *Astrophel and Stella*. Just as he ostentatiously rejects the "phrases fine," the "enameling," and the "strange similes," "the rimes running in rattling rows" and the imitation of "poor Petrarch's long-deceased woes" characteristic of conventional love poetry, so Astrophel throws aside accepted conventions of moral behavior. Poems like the eighteenth sonnet—and there are a great many of them—teach not the sorry consequences that inevitably follow from such rebellion, but rather the delight of it. They show by their own freshness, spontaneity, and explosive energy how invigorating can be the abandonment of the imposed (or ideal) self. As Astrophel tells Love,

> Let *Virtue have that Stella's self; yet thus,*
> *That Virtue but that body grant to us.*
>
> (AS 52)

Astrophel thus detaches the self from the "ethic and politic consideration" with which Sidney, in imitation of Sir Henry, Languet, and the main current of humanistic moral philosophy, had identified it in his letter to Edward Denny. Pretending that the ideal self is only an ideal, Astrophel affirms rather the physical, the sensual, the passionate self—desire and the desired. He intends seduction, aiming to separate Stella's body from her virtue. And he seems to suppose that this can best be accomplished by giving in himself an example of virtue overthrown. In the *Apology* Sidney had criticized English poets for their want of *energia*. Forgetting for the moment that poetry should move men to well-doing, he had complained that, as his contemporaries managed things, it seemed incapable even of moving a woman to bed. Astrophel's purpose is to reinvigorate poetry and thus remedy this defect.

Astrophel and Stella is both the account of a love affair and the instrument of seduction. It tells a story, but is also part of the story. And these two functions depend on one another. The poems hope to persuade *by* narrating, according to a process described in the first lines of the famous first sonnet.

> *Loving in truth, and fain in verse my love to show,*
> *That the dear she might take some pleasure of my pain,*
> *Pleasure might cause her read, reading might make her know,*
> *Knowledge might pity win, and pity grace obtain,*
> *I sought fit words to paint the blackest face of woe.*

Having so neatly outlined his program, Astrophel is stumped. How should he proceed? Where is he to find those "fit words"? He tries study and imitation, but "others' feet still seemed but strangers in my way." Then the answer comes to him, "'Fool,' said my Muse to me, 'look in thy heart and write'." And what, we may ask, does he find in his heart? The image of Stella. His tactic will be to show Stella herself in him. Thus the importance of narration, for what she *is* reveals itself in what he *does*, in the effect she has on him. Seeing herself reflected in him, she will come to know herself, come to know the true nature of her beauty and the end which it should properly serve, and he, in the common courtly euphemism, will "grace obtain." Nor is the theological term wholly inappropriate. The lady, like God (or like Evarchus in the Old *Arcadia*), will grant grace to those who resemble her. By Nature man was created in God's image, and nurture planted in him the image of his father; through love, he is re-created in the likeness of his mistress. "The true love," as Musidorus tells Pyrocles, "hath that excellent nature in it that it doth transform the very essence of the lover into the thing loved." By recounting the story of his re-creation, Astrophel proves that he does love "in truth" and that he is thus worthy "grace." But while demonstrating her power over him, he must exercise his over her. In this consists the art of persuasion and, for Sidney, the art of poetry. Like any good orator who begins a speech by getting the audience on his side, Astrophel must prompt Stella to find in herself the image of his desire—in much the way that the Old *Arcadia* taught the "fair ladies" for whom it was written to recognize something of themselves in the passion of Pyrocles and Musidorus.

The attempted seduction of Stella-Penelope is Sidney's most flagrant abuse of poetry. In the *Apology* he had admitted "that Poesy may not only be abused, but that being abused, by reason of his sweet charming force, it can do more hurt than any other army of words" (Shepherd, p. 125). Yet in *Astrophel and Stella*, as energetic as he makes his verse, it fails. Stella learns to love Astrophel, but rejects his desire. From the moralist's standpoint, this may be vaguely comforting, but even he has little reason to gloat, for Virtue does no better than Desire.

Astrophel and Stella tells not of one, but of two, efforts at persuasion—not only of his attempt to win her to lust, but of hers to win him to virtue. She is the natural book of virtue, the perfect poem as Sidney defined it in the *Defense,* the poem that "setteth virtue so out in her best colors . . . that one must needs be enamoured of her" (Shepherd, p. 111; see pp. 115 and 119). What effect does such a poem really have? Does it teach as well as delight? And does its delightful teaching move to well-doing? These claims that Sidney made for poetry, claims that are the very substance of the *Defense,* are at stake in *Aristrophel and Stella,* for the same claims are made for Stella's beauty. The seventy-first sonnet contains the fullest, though not the only, exploration of them.

> *Who will in fairest book of Nature know,*
> *How virtue may best lodged in beauty be,*
> *Let him but learn of Love to read in thee,*
> *Stella, those fair lines, which true goodness show.*
> *There shall he find all vices' overthrow,*
> *Not by rude force, but sweetest sovereignty*
> *Of reason, from whose light those night-birds fly,*
> *That inward sun in thine eyes shineth so.*

> *And not content to be Perfection's heir*
> *Thyself, doest strive all minds that way to move,*
> *Who mark in thee what is in thee most fair.*
> *So while thy beauty draws the heart to love,*
> *As fast thy virtue draws that love to good.*

Reduce these lines to prose and make of the "fairest book of Nature" some actual book, and they would not be out of place in the *Apology for Poetry*. But there Sidney leaves out, as I have done here, the last line, "But ah, Desire still cries, 'Give me some food.' "[30] Her attempt at persuasion is no more successful than his. She discovers in him, as he does in her, an unpersuadable self. Her beauty sparks his desire, but her virtue is unable to bend that desire to good. Such, we are left to conclude, might well be the effect of a poem constructed according to the same formula, a poem that dared incite passion in the interest of well-doing.

So many readers, both in Sidney's time and in ours, have found in his poetry a vindication of his *Defence* that I think it fair to ask whether its Platonic optimism accurately describes the experience of *Astrophel and Stella*, or, for that matter, the experience of the Old *Arcadia*. The young men who see Virtue in the form of a beautiful woman are indeed "wonderfully ravished with the love of her," but are they moved to virtuous action? Or, on the contrary, does the antiromantic pessimism of Sidney's last days better describe their experience? Is beauty more apt to allure them "to evil than to frame any good in them"? If we adopt the point of view of Sir Henry, of Languet, of Evarchus, the point of view of Reason itself as Sidney understood it, there can be little doubt about the answer. Pyrocles, Musidorus, and Astrophel each gain our sympathy but are otherwise not much improved by their contact with beauty. The point of view is admittedly narrow. Had Sidney not rebelled against it, his name would today be unknown. But though we admire the idealism of the *Defense*, enjoy the witty realism of Astrophel, and deplore the lugubrious morality of Sidney repentant, the three belong together. The first makes a claim for poetry; the second tests it; and the third makes a judgment that could well have been based on that test. But before Sidney got to the point of final judgment, he did try to write a poem that would accomplish all that the *Defense* claimed, a poem that any but the severest humanist might approve. That poem is, of course, the revised *Arcadia*.

The first pages of the New *Arcadia* portray a passion unlike any we have known in Sidney. In the Old *Arcadia* Pyrocles defended his affection with the vaguely Platonic commonplace that it fed his mind with higher thoughts, but his actions belied his philosophy. Strephon and Klaius, the first characters we meet in the New *Arcadia*, have truly been made better by love. Though they had been "silly ignorant shepherds," now "great clerks do not disdain [their] conference." The effect of love amazes them and should, after our reading of the Old *Arcadia* and *Astrophel and Stella*, amaze us. "Hath not the desire to seem worthy in [Urania's] eyes made us, when others were sleeping, to sit viewing the course of the heavens? When others were running at base, to run over learned writings? When others mark their sheep, we to mark ourselves? Hath not she thrown reason upon our desires, and, as it were, given eyes unto Cupid? Hath in any but in her, love-fellowship maintained friendship between rivals, and beauty taught the beholders chastity?" (Feuillerat, I, 7–8). We learn, however, of their extraordinary love only to learn of their bereavement. Urania, in whom we recognize the celestial Venus, has left the world.[31] And the place on the shore where she was last seen is soon to be taken by the half-drowned Musidorus, a victim of "human inhumanity." Even in the revised version, Arcadia is no pagan Garden of Eden. It is a fallen world, but one that has been and perhaps can again be touched by a love that turns desire to welldoing.

The same set of abstract terms—Beauty, Virtue, Desire, and the rest—which occurs so regularly elsewhere in Sidney dominates the New *Arcadia*, though with an altered emphasis. The New *Arcadia* approaches the optimism of the *Defense of Poesy*, without, however, the *Defense's* self-depreciating irony. Indeed, one of the first things we notice in the New *Arcadia* is the disappearance of an identifiable narrator. With rare exceptions (uncorrected leftovers from the earlier version), the story tells itself or gets told by some one or another of the characters within it. The style is no longer that of a person speaking, as it was in the Old *Arcadia*, in the *Defense*, or in *Astrophel and Stella*, but rather than of a speaking picture. Neither accomplice nor judge, it sets forth in the fairest and most flattering colors the virtuous beauties and beauteous virtues of its various protagonists. Gone are the asides to the "fair ladies," and gone too (at least as a prominent figure) is the author's most evident surrogate, Philisides. Sidney thus withdraws the invitation which before he had so generously extended—the invitation to see the author portrayed in his work. Here he tries rather to create a romantic fiction that will be acceptable not for his sake, not out of mere partiality, but for its intrinsic merit.

There are, of course, other changes, most of them tending to exculpate Pyrocles and Musidorus. We learn more of their heroic adventures and less, if the bowdlerization of the incompletely revised last books is authorial, of their amorous misadventures.[32] Musidorus does not undertake the rape of Pamela, and Pyrocles does not consummate his love of Philoclea. Nor is love any longer the principal cause of misfortune. The bear and the lion in Book One, the Phagonian rebellion in Book Two, and the captivity in Book Three all derive from the malignant ambition of Cecropia, a new character in the revised *Arcadia*. The early version had no villain. Blame belonged solely to love and to Basilius's foolish retirement. In the New *Arcadia* Basilius is still at fault, but love is not. The presence of Pyrocles and Musidorus does nothing to prompt Cecropia, and in their absence she would have been successful. Love does, however, disrupt order in many of the subsidiary episodes, yet even these set Pyrocles and Musidorus off to advantage, either by showing the possibility of an ideal love, as in the story of Argalus and Parthenia, or by showing a passion so distinctly inferior to theirs that they seem admirable by contrast, as in the case of Erona and Antiphilus. Something of the new attitude toward love can be seen in Pyrocles' comment on Queen Helen, whose passion for Amphialus had cost the lives of Philoxenus and Timotheus. "You may see by her example (in herself wise, and of others beloved) that neither folly is the cause of vehement love, nor reproach the effect. For never, I think, was there any woman that with a more unremoveable determination gave herself to the counsel of love . . . and yet is neither her wisdom doubted of, nor honor blemished" (Feuillerat, I, 283–284). If the object of love is worthy, then the love itself is blameless whatever its consequences.

The New *Arcadia* seemingly comes much closer than did the Old to achieving exemplary moral clarity. As Sidney argued in the *Apology*, "If the poet do his part aright, he will show you in Tantulus, Atreus, and such like, nothing that is not to be shunned; in Cyrus, Aeneas, Ulysses, each thing to be followed" (Shepherd, p. 110). Yet Sidney curiously upsets the nice arrangement of good and evil that he recommended and had been at such pains to secure. As guilt shifts to Cecropia, and as the young protagonists become unambiguously praiseworthy, our interest moves away from them to Amphialus. He, not Pyrocles or Musidorus, Pamela, Philoclea, or Cecropia, is the central figure in the third book of the New *Arcadia*. And he is a character neither wholly good nor wholly bad—one in whom there is much to be followed and much more to be shunned. What is more, he, like Pyrocles and Musidorus in the first books of the Old *Arcadia*, condemns his own actions, yet is powerless to change them. Sidney's artistic sense explains in part the prominence of this new character. As good and evil took their respective sides of the stage, the center was left vacant. But I think too that a more intimate concern motivated him. With the moral polarization of the *Arcadia*, the issue that most excited his imagination, the torment of a mind divided against itself, disappeared. The story might now be exemplary, but it was no longer true to his experience, to that experience which lies so close to the surface of his other works. This, of course, is only a guess, but it is supported by at least one otherwise inexplicable fact, that Amphialus betrays something of the autobiographical coloring that had distinguished Pyrocles, Musidorus, Philisides, Astrophel, and the speaker of the *Defense*. Amphialus takes over the song in which Philisides had told of the genesis of his love; he replaces the Old *Arcadia*'s narrator in his devotion to Philoclea; and he is the disappointed heir of his uncle as Philip

Sidney was the disappointed heir of his. Moreover, Sidney and Amphialus are, as Kenneth Myrick has written, "alike in courtesy, in energetic leadership, in courage and skill in tourney, perhaps in melancholy."[33] Now this evidence, all of the unreliable type five,[34] is hardly sufficient to identify Sidney with Amphialus. Nor is there much in it to suggest that such recognition was an intended part of our response. The personal coloring is faint and little attention is drawn to it. The New *Arcadia* is largely bereft of those sly and knowing winks in the direction of the sympathetic reader that abound in the early version or in *Astrophel and Stella*. Yet Amphialus's predicament, that of a man who for beauty does what he knows wrong, so resembles that of those other protagonists in whom we *are* invited to see the author, that we presume the predicament was in some measure Sidney's own. Despite his moralization and objectification, he could not keep this issue from finding its way into the New *Arcadia*.

Book Three of the New *Arcadia* represents a crisis in Sidney's literary career. Where the first two books followed, though with frequent digression, the plot of the early version, the third strikes out on its own. This single episode, itself nearly two-thirds as long as the five books of the Old *Arcadia*, is Sidney's most concerted attempt to satisfy in literature the demands made on him by his station and upbringing, his most thorough application in practice of the aesthetic doctrines that he had preached in the *Defense*. Yet Book Three leads nowhere. Rather it exhausts most of the material that had remade the *Arcadia*. Cecropia dies, and her heir in villainy, Anaxius, seems to be nearing his end as the book breaks off. Amphialus too has been brought to the verge of death and, though it appears likely that he will be cured both physically and morally by Queen Helen, he has been effectively removed from the story. The Erona intrigue from Book Two remains unfinished, but it could hardly be made to play the polarizing role that Cecropia had in the first three books. No, had Sidney continued the New *Arcadia*, he would have had to do something very like what the Countess of Pembroke did in the edition of 1593; he would have had to return to the old plot.

As inevitable as sin or death, the pattern of the Old *Arcadia*, which is also the pattern of education drama and of Euphuistic

fiction, is built into the New. The scene of admonition is dis-
located, fragmented, and dispersed, but it is there, and it sets up an
expectation of eventual judgment, an expectation that Sidney
apparently intended to satisfy, as he had done before, with a trial
of the two young princes, a trial presided over by Evarchus. The
Oracle's pronouncement to Basilius proves that as late as the
closing pages of Book Two, Sidney's plan was unchanged. He
retained the reference to Evarchus ("In thy own seat a foreign state
shall sit"), and added one to Pyrocles and Musidorus ("Who at
thy bier, as at a bar, shall plead"). Could the old pattern of admonition, rebellion, and judgment, however elaborately reworked, be
made to yield a new meaning? Sidney's attempt closely resembles
that of the Euphuists in the pastoral romances of the late 'eighties,
an attempt to escape the implications of the pattern without abandoning it. But Sidney had created in Evarchus a more severe judge
than any the Euphuists had to encounter. Would the changes he
had made in the story compel that upright old man to change his
judgment? I don't think so. Nor do I think that Sidney would have
dismissed Evarchus's judgment as easily as do modern critics.
That judgment derived from a set of assumptions so unquestion-
ably true that no amount of Platonizing sympathy with beauty and
its effects could overturn it.

Why was the New *Arcadia* left unfinished? In Thomas Moffet's
sixteenth-century life of Sidney, there is a clue that modern critics
have not been eager to credit. After admitting that Sidney amused
himself with literature "after the manner of youth, but within
limits," Moffet goes on,

*he was somewhat wanton, indeed, but observed a measure and felt shame.
On that account he first consigned his* Stella *(truly an elegant and
pleasant work) to darkness and then favored giving it to fire. Nay, more, he
desired to smother the* Arcadia *(offspring of no ill pen) at the time of its
birth. . . . Having come to fear . . . that his* Stella *and his* Arcadia *might
render the souls of readers more yielding instead of better, and having
turned to worthier subjects, he very much wished to sing something which
would abide the censure of the most austere Cato.*[35]

Out of moral compunction, Sidney "turned to worthier subjects" (*ad digniora conversus argumenta*), to his translations, as
Moffet tells us, of "the *Week* of the great Bartas" and "the

psalms of the Hebrew poet." Might such compunction explain the abrupt abandonment of the New *Arcadia*?

So far as I know, no modern interpreter of Sidney has thought so. Critics and biographers alike have rather ignored this side of Sidney. So eager have they been to explain the nature of his success—a success which they, like many of his contemporaries, simply assume—that they have been unwilling to consider even the possibility that in his own eyes Sidney had failed. They mention the evidence of his literary repentance, if at all, only to deny it. For example, a recent editor of the Sidnean Psalms dismisses Moffet with the disparaging remark that his "chronology . . . provides for his purpose a convenient moral pattern."[36] We assume that because Moffet's arrangement fits a moral pattern it must be false. An Elizabethan would have taken the opposite view. Because it fit, he would have assumed it was true, for the pattern was, as those who rebelled against it sooner or later discovered, itself a true model of human experience.

But neither our assumption nor theirs should be accepted without corroboration. What evidence have we? Moffet and Greville agree that at some point, whether on his deathbed or several years earlier, Sidney determined that his literary works "might render the souls of readers more yielding instead of better." I think their testimony credible. When they wrote there were many, including Sidney's brother, sister, and widow, who could have, and probably would have, contradicted their account had it not been true. As it is, the first printed reference to Sidney's request that the *Arcadia* be burned makes Lady Sidney the one who reported it, and Moffet says that it was Robert Sidney himself who received his brother's dying wish that his "Anacreontics" not see the light. Moreover, though it includes no mention of a specifically literary repentance, the report of George Gifford, the minister who attended on Sidney in his last illness, agrees in tone with the other accounts. According to Gifford, Sidney condemned "all things in [his] former life" as "vain, vain, vain," and in particular he renounced his love for Penelope Rich. "I had this night a trouble in my mind," Sidney told Gifford. "For searching myself, methought I had not a full and sure hold in Christ. After I had continued in this perplexity a while, observe how strangely God did deliver me—for indeed it was a strange deliverance that I had! There came to my remembrance a vanity wherein I had taken delight, whereof I had not rid myself. It was my Lady Rich. But I rid myself of it, and presently my joy and comfort returned."[37] Sidney does here what long before, under the serio-comic guise of Astrophel, he had claimed he would do, but in the *Astrophel and Stella* never quite did.

> Virtue, awake! Beauty but beauty is.
> I may, I must, I can, I will, I do
> Leave following that which it is gain to miss.
>
> (AS 47)

It was not only on his deathbed that he discovered that the vanity which had inspired his best verse weakened his hold on Christ, nor was it only there that he learned to fear the effect that his writing might have on its readers. The question is: Did such a discovery or such a fear lead him to some earlier repentance? Did it perhaps prompt him to abandon the New *Arcadia*?

We have seen that, when Sidney broke it off, the New *Arcadia* was heading back toward an inevitable confrontation with justice, a confrontation that would, in all likelihood, have resulted in the same division of sympathy from judgment that characterized the Old *Arcadia*. And we have noticed too that, even in what he had written so far, Sidney was either unable or unwilling to maintain the exemplary distinction of good from evil which he recommended in the *Defense*. Furthermore, a new interest invades the third book of the revised *Arcadia*. In Pamela's refutation of atheism, there is an excess that testifies to Sidney's own passionate concern for theology. The most recent chronology of his life includes this entry under 1583: "Suspended work on the New *Arcadia* and began translating Du Mornay's *Truth of Religion*."[38] Perhaps Moffet's "moral pattern" was true; perhaps Sidney did turn from romance "to worthier subjects." The dates are not conclusive, but it is now commonly thought that he abandoned the *Arcadia* a year or more before he was appointed governor of Flushing, and there is at least some evidence to suggest that his translations of Du Plessis Mornay, of the Psalms, and of Du Bartas belong to the intervening period.[39]

Why did Sidney break off the *Arcadia*? Because no romantic fiction could placate the Evarchuses of the world, nor could it placate the Evarchus within, the voice of Sidney's own conscience. On the other hand, a treatise in defense of the Christian religion, the Psalms of David, or a versified account of the Creation could. And how might Sidney more effectively have removed himself and his unruly desires from his work than by turning to translation? Though it is not what we we expect from the mirror of English chivalry in an age of courtly poets, Sidney, like Gascoigne, Lodge, or Greene, repented. "Leave me, O Love, which reachest but to dust," does not, as some nineteenth-century editors liked to think, belong to Astrophel. But it does belong to Sidney. His life has rather the closed and conventional shape of the *Certain Sonnets* than the open-ended design of the two *Arcadia*s or *Astrophel and Stella*, the inconclusive but intriguing works of his rebellion.

For Sidney, as for many of his contemporaries, the period of rebellion was a period of testing. From 1578 to 1584, during those six frustrating years between his embassy to Germany and his appointment as governor of Flushing, years when, deprived of office, he was kept from satisfying expectation in the usual way, Sidney tested poetry—and all that was associated with it—love, beauty, contemplation, and desire—against the humanists' standard of rational well-doing. And poetry failed. It could neither be reconciled to the paternal notion of virtue, nor could it stand on its own as an alternative system of value. Sidney backed down in his *Defense of Poesy* at the crucial moment, just when the attack turned against what he and his contemporaries actually wrote. And his other works do no better. The Old *Arcadia* shows youthful passion unable to answer the judgment of age; *Astrophel and Stella* reveals the corrupting effect of beauty; and the New *Arcadia* abandons in midsentence its uncompleted attempt to erect a fictional image of heroic love. Sidney did try to broaden the scope of humanistic values, to achieve that "larger and richer humanism" with which Kenneth Myrick and the world generally has credited him.[40] But given his earnest desire to satisfy the expectations of men like Sir Henry Sidney and Hubert Languet, the task proved impossible. He was too good and too serious a son and pupil to defend successfully values hostile to what he had been taught. As a result his tone is constantly, though engagingly, self-depreciating.

We would better understand that tone, Sidney himself, and perhaps his literary generation, if we took the *Defense* from its honored place on the shelf near Aristotle's *Poetics* and put it somewhat closer to *The Praise of Folly*. It belongs with the paradoxical encomia. The Count of Hanau, Sidney's continental friend, traveling companion, and correspondent—a young man like Sidney in both intellect and inclination, according to Languet, who fostered their friendship and directed each—expressed the more usual view, the view supposed by Sidney's letter to Denny, in a Latin oration entitled, "The Study of Profane Literature is Altogether Unnecessary for a Prince."[41] Sir Henry or Languet would perhaps not have put it so bluntly, but they would surely have agreed that a serious and sustained commitment to poetry was unworthy a man of their class and breeding. Half accepting this view, even as they rebelled against it, Sidney and many of the other gentleman-writers of his generation found it natural to represent themselves as prodigals. The pattern of prodigality supplied a mask for rebellion, a role that could be played all the more exuberantly because it was destined to end in defeat. For if their own unruly desires or the "unnoble constitution of [their] time"[42] kept them from fulfilling the positive expectations of their fathers and teachers, if they could not make an important contribution to the commonweal, they could nevertheless still satisfy negative expectation, the expectation that prodigality leads to repentance. They could rebel, suffer guilt, and repent, and thus acquire an identity supported by the governing ethos of their age. The pattern of rebellion, guilt, and repentance was a guarantee of achieved selfhood for so many of these writers—a mirror in which they found a reflection of their works and lives—that we may, not unfairly, call them a generation of prodigals.

Notes

Abbreviations

ELR   *English Literary Renaissance*

HLQ   *Huntington Library Quarterly*

MLR   *Modern Language Review*

NLH   *New Literary History*

PQ   *Philological Quarterly*

RES   *Review of English Studies*

SEL   *Studies in English Literature*

SQ   *Shakespeare Quarterly*

UMEES   University Microfilms, Early English Series

Notes

1: PATTERNS OF PRODIGALITY

1. Princeton, 1969.
2. Wilson, "Euphues and the Prodigal Son," *The Library*, 10 (1909), 337–361.
3. *Sir Walter Raleigh: The Renaissance Man and his Roles* (New Haven, 1973).
4. Fraser's *War Against Poetry* (Princeton, 1970) explores the Elizabethan emphasis on thrift and labor, and the concurrent antipathy to poetry; and his *Dark Ages and the Age of Gold* (Princeton, 1973) examines the defensiveness of the poets themselves. Though I regard the attitudes of the Elizabethans with greater sympathy than does Fraser, we agree with each other and disagree with almost every other critic who has written about this period in our understanding of what those attitudes were.
5. I am thinking, of course, of Harold Bloom, *The Anxiety of Influence* (New York, 1973), and Walter Jackson Bate, *The Burden of the Past and the English Poet* (Cambridge, Mass., 1970).
6. *The Rocke of Regard* (1576), sig. ¶ ii^v. (UMEES, Reel 553.)
7. *Rocke of Regard*, sig. ¶ iii^v.
8. Printed with Kendall's *Flowers of Epigrammes* by the Spenser Society (1874; rpt. New York, 1967), p. 243.
9. *The Rise of the Novel* (Berkeley and Los Angeles, 1957), p. 28.
10. *Euphues*, ed. Morris William Croll and Harry Clemons (1916; rpt. New York, 1964), p. 10.
11. There are certain obvious ways in which Lyly was not like Euphues: for one, he was not rich, and, for another, he did not return to "Athens" to become "public reader in the University, with such commendation as never any before him," though perhaps he hoped to do so.
12. See William Nelson, *Fact or Fiction: The Dilemma of the Renaissance Storyteller* (Cambridge, Mass., 1973).
13. See Albert Feuillerat, *John Lyly* (Cambridge, 1910), pp. 274–275, and G. K. Hunter, *John Lyly: The Humanist as Courtier* (London, 1962), p. 41.
14. "The 'Fluellenian' Method," *PMLA*, 90 (1975), 292. This is Levin's reply to criticisms of his earlier article, "On Fluellen's Figures, Christ Figures, and James Figures," *PMLA*, 89 (1974), 302–311. The criticisms appeared in *PMLA*, 90 (1975), 117–120.
15. *Letters from Petrarch*, selected and trans. Morris Bishop (Bloomington, Ind., 1966), p. 5.
16. As well as being a commonplace of historical novels, historical movies, and even a good many older histories, the Marlovian vision governs the one "generational history" of these men, Anthony Esler's

The Aspiring Mind of the Elizabethan Younger Generation (Durham, N.C., 1966).

17. These three periods correspond in a general way to those discerned by J. W. H. Atkins in his discussion of the history of Elizabethan prose fiction in the *Cambridge History of English Literature* (Cambridge, 1909), III, 387–388.

18. "Histoires et sciences sociales; La longue durée," *Annales; Économies, sociétés, civilisations,* 13 (1958), 725–753.

2: THE MIRROR OF DUTY

1. On Lyly's family and education see Albert Feuillerat, *John Lyly,* pp. 3–40, and G. K. Hunter, *John Lyly: The Humanist as Courtier* (London, 1962), pp. 17–30 and 36–48.

2. On Gascoigne see C. T. Prouty, *George Gascoigne: Elizabethan Courtier, Soldier, and Poet* (New York, 1942), pp. 315–324; on Lodge see Edward Andrews Tenney, *Thomas Lodge* (1935; rpt. New York, 1969), pp. 87–90.

3. *The Life and Complete Works of Robert Greene,* ed. Alexander B. Grosart, 15 vols. (1881–1883; rpt. New York, 1964), XII, 161 and 171.

4. Reprined in James M. Osborne, *Young Philip Sidney, 1572– 1577* (New Haven, 1972), pp. 11–13.

5. *Ad Demonicum,* trans. John Bury (1557), sig. b v. (UMEES, Reel 468).

6. The influence of the *Ad Demonicum* on Elizabethan literature has been briefly surveyed by G. K. Hunter, "Isocrates' Precepts and Polonius' Character," *SQ,* 8 (1957), 501–506.

7. "Sir Walter Raleigh's *Instructions to his Son,"* in *Elizabethan and Jacobean Studies Presented to Frank Percy Wilson* (Oxford, 1959), p. 199.

8. *Advice to a Son,* ed. Louis B. Wright (Ithaca, 1962), p. 32.

9. Grosart, IX, 137. Of the sentence in Raleigh, Latham remarks, "At the very end he brings his reading of life suddenly and characteristically under the eye of God, and we see how much of *contemptus mundi* there has been in this worldly wisdom" (p. 216). This is no less true for the fact that Raleigh's "reading of life" was aided either by his reading of Greene, or, as I suppose is more probable, by his reading of their common source, whatever it may have been.

10. Wright, p. 9.

11. *The Schoolmaster,* ed. Lawrence V. Ryan (Ithaca, 1967), p. 115.

12. Osborne, p. 14.

13. Quoted by Kenneth Charlton, *Education in Renaissance England* (London, 1965), p. 80.

14. *Educational Charters and Documents, 598 to 1909,* ed. Arthur F. Leach (1911; rpt. New York, 1971), p. 470.

15. "The Educational Revolution in England, 1560–1640," *Past and Present,* no. 28 (1964), 41–80.

16. The squeeze may have been due in part to a general rise in population. As John R. Gillis has observed, "In times of population

growth, when there were larger numbers of children than usual, even more younger sons and daughters were cut loose to pursue uncertain futures in towns or rural frontier areas. We know that this happened in the period 1550–1630, when the English population doubled. . . . Contemporaries believed that they detected growing generational tensions, and there were moves to tighten the authority of the heads of households, workshops, and schools against the 'defections and revolts in children of lewd behavior, which have contemptuously prophaned all obedience to parents.' " *Youth and History: Tradition and Change in European Age Relations, 1770-Present* (New York, 1974), pp. 18–19. The demographic pressure would have particularly affected the upper classes, which, according to Stone, "trebled at a period when the total population barely doubled." "Social Mobility in England, 1500–1700," *Past and Present*, no. 33 (1966), 23–24.

17. Hunter, *Lyly*, p. 34. Mark H. Curtis has discussed the political and social effects of this frustration on the next several generations of university graduates in "The Alienated Intellectuals of Early Stuart England," *Past and Present*, no. 23 (1962), 25–41.

18. *The Correspondence of Sir Philip Sidney and Hubert Languet*, trans. and ed. Steuart A. Pears (London, 1845), p. 143.

19. Osborne, p. 537.

20. From Whetstone's *Remembrance of Gascoigne*, quoted by Prouty, p. 99. Gascoigne died in Whetstone's Stamford home, so Whetstone's testimony may be supposed to have some weight. The advice, in any case, closely resembles what we find in several of Gascoigne's poems, his "Counsel to Douglas Dive" and his "Counsel given to Master Bartholomew Withypoll," both in *The Posies*.

21. Grosart, XII, 171.

22. Joan Simon, *Education and Society in Tudor England* (Cambridge, 1967), p. 363.

23. Cf. Pettie's opinion that learning is "only it which maketh you gentlemen." *The Civile Conversation of M. Steeven Guazzo*, ed. Sir Edward Sullivan, 2 vols. (London, 1925), I, 9.

24. Starkey, *Dialogue*, ed. K. M. Burton (London, 1948), p. 22.

25. *Ibid.*, p. 24.

26. Fritz Caspari, *Humanism and the Social Order in Tudor England* (1954; rpt. New York, 1968), p. 218.

27. Bryskett, *Discourse*, ed. Thomas E. Wright (Northridge, Calif., 1970), p. 9.

28. *Ibid.*, p. 16.

29. *Ibid.*, p. 23.

30. *Ibid.*, p. 22.

31. *Ibid.*, p. 21.

32. Osborne, pp. 537–538.

33. *The Rocke of Regard*, sig. ¶ ii^v. (UMEES, Reel 553.)

34. *The Renaissance Discovery of Time* (Cambridge, Mass., 1972), pp. 189–199.

35. Leach, p. 519. Cf. the similar regulations at Merchant Taylors' School reprinted in F.W. Draper, *Four Centuries of Merchant Taylors' School* (Oxford, 1962), Appendix I.

36. Lawrence Stone, *The Crisis of the Aristocracy, 1558–1641* (Oxford, 1965), pp. 679–680.

37. Pears, p. 25.

38. *Nugae Antiquae*, ed. Henry Harington and Thomas Park, 2 vols. (London, 1804), I, 131–135.

39. See Gordon J. Schochet, "Patriarchalism, Politics and Mass Attitudes in Stuart England," *The Historical Journal*, 12 (1969), 413–441. Peele's letter is reprinted in David H. Horne, *The Life and Minor Works of George Peele* (New Haven, 1952), pp. 105. Philoplutos, who represents Burghley in Lodge's *Catharos*, calls himself *Pater patriae*. *The Complete Works of Thomas Lodge*, ed. E.W. Gosse, 4 vols. (1993; rpt New York, 1963), II, 8.

40. Simon, pp. 227–228, 233, 242, 266, 305, 309, 310n, 311, and 315.

41. Stone, *Crisis*, pp. 679–680 and 693–694.

42. Hunter, *Lyly*, p. 72.

43. *Ibid.*, p. 69.

44. Prouty, pp. 93, 95, and 234; and Thomas C. Izard, *George Whetstone: Mid-Elizabethan Gentleman of Letters* (New York, 1942), pp. 9–10.

45. Horne, p. 108.

46. Quoted by B. W. Beckingsale, *Burghley: Tudor Statesman* (London, 1967), p. 253.

47. Lodge, *Catharos*, Gosse, II, 63; and Spenser, "The Ruines of Time," 11. 440–455. On Burghley's patronage see Beckingsale, pp. 226 ff. and 245–269.

48. Richard Jacob Panofsky, "A Descriptive Study of English Mid-Tudor Short Poetry, 1557–1577" (Ph.D. diss., University of California, Santa Barbara, 1975), p. 7.

49. Elyot, *The Book named the Governor*, ed. S. E. Lehmberg (London, 1962), pp. 28–40.

50. In the words of Walter J. Ong, S.J., *Rhetoric, Romance, and Technology* (Ithaca, 1971), p. 129.

51. Compare Osborne, pp. 538–540, and Pears, p. 26.

52. Elyot, p. 47.

53. *Ibid.*, p. 48, and Ascham, p. 143.

54. "Nor truly would I yield Terence this room," writes Humphrey, "but for I saw Cicero so much esteem him who took not the least part of eloquence of him, like Chysostom of Aristophanes." *The Nobles or of Nobilitye* (1563), sig. y iii^v. (UMEES, Reel 249.) Humphrey presided over Magdalen College, Oxford, when Lyly was a student there.

55. *Th' Overthrow of Stage-Playes*, ed. Arthur Freeman (New York, 1974), pp. 121–125.

56. See William Ringler, "The Immediate Source of Euphuism," *PMLA*, 53 (1938), 678–686; and Ringler, *Stephen Gosson: A Biographical and Critical Study* (Princeton, 1942), pp. 10–15 and 76.

57. Croll and Clemons, p. 143.

58. *Orlando Furioso* (1591), sig. Mm ii. (UMEES, Reel 194.)

59. Spenser's *English Poet* has not survived, but E. K. provides a clue to its contents in his headnote to the October Eclogue of *The Shepheardes Calender*.

60. Descriptions and discussions of these plays are to be found in
C.H. Herford, *Studies in the Literary Relations between England and Germany in the Sixteenth Century* (Cambridge, 1886), pp. 87–90 and
149—164; R.W. Bond, *Early Plays from the Italian* (Oxford, 1911), pp. xci-cix; T. W. Baldwin, *Shakspere's Five-Act Structure* (Urbana, Ill., 1947),
pp. 242–251; Marvin Herrick, *Tragicomedy* (1955; rpt. Urbana, 1962),
pp. 37-46; and F. P. Wilson, *The English Drama, 1485-1585* (Oxford,
1969), pp. 96–101.

61. See Ong, "Latin Language Study as Renaissance Puberty Rite,"
in *Rhetoric, Romance, and Technology,* pp. 113–141.

62. *De Pueris Instituendis*, trans. W. H. Woodward in *Erasmus, Concerning the Aims and Methods of Education* (1904; rpt. New York, 1964),
p. 189. The next sentences refer to Erasmus' *Peregrinatio Religionis Ergo,* a
colloquy that was particularly well known in England.

63. See C. L. Barber, " 'The Form of Faustus' Fortunes Good or
Bad,' " *The Tulane Drama Review,* 8 (1964), 92–119.

64. Pears, p. 6.

65. Published in Antwerp in 1529, *Acolastus* went through more
than forty-eight editions in sixty years. It was performed at Cambridge
and at Winchester School; it was translated into English in a version
especially intended for classroom use, by John Palsgrave, a schoolmaster and sometimes tutor to Princess Mary; and it retained at least a
certain currency through the end of the century. In 1594 Nashe
irreverently described a performance in his *Unfortunate Traveler,* and in
1600 Samuel Nicholson used the name of its protagonist in his poem of
satire and repentance, *Acolastus his After-Wit.*

66. *Acolastus,* trans. W. E. D. Atkinson, *University of Western Ontario
Studies in the Humanities,* 3 (1964), 111–113.

67. *English Morality Plays and Moral Interludes,* ed. Edgar T. Schell
and J. D. Schuchter (New York, 1969), p. 201.

68. I explore the relation of *Hamlet* to these traditions in "What
Hamlet Remembers," *Shakespeare Studies,* 10 (forthcoming).

69. Pears, p. 6; Ascham, pp. 61–68.

70. R. Willis, quoted by David Bevington, *From Mankind to Marlowe*
(Cambridge, Mass., 1962), pp. 13–14.

71. *The Countess of Pembroke's Arcadia (The Old Arcadia),* ed. Jean
Robertson (Oxford, 1973), pp. 28–29. See also p. 40.

72. Grosart, IX, 163.

73. *Orlando Furioso,* sig. Mm iii.

74. *Orlando Furioso,* sig. ¶ viii-viii^v.

75. *Rocke of Regard,* sig. ¶ ii^v.

76. *Queen Elizabeth I: A Biography* (1934; rpt. New York, 1957), p. 313.

77. Simon, p. 401. Cf. Kenneth Charlton: "If a man like Sir William
Cecil came nearest to the ideal which Elyot sought, Sidney, Spenser
and Raleigh owe more to Castiglione." (p. 83).

78. Kenneth Myrick, *Sir Philip Sidney as Literary Craftsman* (1935; rpt.
Lincoln, Neb., 1965), p. 21.

79. Hunter, *Lyly,* p. 61.

80. Elyot, pp. 33 and 39.
81. *Euphues*, ed. Croll and Clemons, p. 200.

3: GASCOIGNE

1. *The Complete Works of George Gascoigne*, ed. John W. Cunliffe, 2 vols. (Cambridge, 1907), II, 135. Subsequent references to this edition will appear in the text.
2. *A Hundreth Sundrie Flowres*, ed. C. T. Prouty (1942; rpt. Columbia, Mo. 1970), p. 57.
3. *Ibid.*, p. 105.
4. The one exception to this rule is Gascoigne's last work, *The Grief of Joy* (1576), dedicated to Queen Elizabeth. Based on Petrarch's *De remedius utriusque fortunae*, it does relate each of its four dissections of human vanity ("the griefs or discommodities of lusty youth," "the vanity of beauty," "the faults of force and strength," and "the vanities of activities") to his own experiences. This slight relenting, which is accompanied by a more genial tone, may, as Prouty suggests, have been due to a suspicion that "the heavy-handed asceticism of *The Droomme of Doomes* day or *A delicate Diet* would not meet with royal favor" as readily as something a bit less austere. See *George Gascoigne: Elizabethan Courtier, Soldier, and Poet* (New York, 1942), pp. 263–264.
5. Prouty, *Gascoigne*, pp. 93–96.
6. Erasmus, *Paraphrase upon the Newe Testament* (1548), and Cornelius à Lapide, *The Great Commentary*, trans. T. W. Mossman (London, 1892), St. Luke's Gospel, p. 372. It should be noted that the Prodigal's reputation for quick wit accompanied his allegorical identification with the Gentiles and thus, for Erasmus in particular, with the wise pagans of antiquity.
7. *The Schoolmaster (1570)*, ed. Lawrence V. Ryan (Ithaca, N.Y., 1967), pp. 21 and 23. Cf. *Institutio Oratoria*, I, iii, 1–5. Ryan compares the two works in some detail in *Roger Ascham* (Stanford, Calif., 1963), pp. 262–265. Subsequent references to Ryan's edition of *The Schoolmaster* will appear in the text.
8. *De Ingenius Moribus*, trans. W. H. Woodward, in *Vittorino da Feltra and Other Humanist Educators* (Cambridge, 1897), p. 109.
9. *De Anima et Vita* (Basel, 1538), sig. H 1.
10. See Bernhard Blumenkranz, "Siliquae Porcorum, L'exégèse médiévale et les sciences profanes," *Mélanges d'Histoire du Moyen Age, dédiés á la mémoire de Louis Halphen* (Paris, 1951), pp. 11–17.

4: LYLY

1. *The Complete Works of John Lyly*, ed. R. Warwick Bond, 3 vols. (Oxford, 1902), I, 65–71.

2. *Pierces Supererogation* in *The Works of Gabriel Harvey*, ed. Alexander B. Grosart, 3 vols. (London, 1884–1885), II, 128.

3. Anthony Munday, *Zelauto . . . Given . . . to Euphues* (1580), Barnabe Rich, *The Second Tome of the Travailes and Adventures of Don Simonides* (1584), Greene, *Euphues his Censure to Philautus* (1587) and *Menaphon Camillas Alarum to Slumbering Euphues* (1589), and Lodge, *Rosalynde. Euphues Golden Legacie* (1590) and *Euphues Shadow* (1592).

4. Rich, *The Second Tome*, sig. I iv. (UMEES, Reel 393.)

5. *Ibid.*, sig. I iii.

6. Gosse's *Lodge*, II, 8.

7. *Second Tome*, sig. A iv.

8. Gosse, II, 8.

9. Wallace A. Bacon in his introduction to William Warner's *Syrinx* (1950; rpt. New York, 1970), p. xlviii.

10. Samuel Gardiner, *Portraiture of the Prodigal Sonne* (1599), sig. A4^V-A5. (UMEES, Reel 243.)

11. *Euphues: The Anatomy of Wit and his England*, ed. Morris W. Croll and Harry Clemons (1916; rpt. New York, 1964), p. 191. References in the text to *Euphues* will be to this edition.

12. John Dover Wilson, "Euphues and the Prodigal Son," *The Library*, 10 (1909), 337–361.

13. William Ringler, "The Immediate Source of Euphuism," *PMLA*, 53 (1938), 678–686.

14. For a suggestive analysis of Lyly's antithetical style, see Jonas Barish, "The Prose Style of John Lyly," *ELH*, 23 (1956), 14–35.

15. *Experientia stultorium magistra*. The free translation is Ascham's (*Schoolmaster*, ed. Ryan, p. 51).

16. Walter R. Davis, *Idea and Act in Elizabethan Fiction* (Princeton, 1969), p. 119. Cf. G. K. Hunter who argues that the letters with which *Euphues* concludes show "experience as the true teacher of a ready wit" (*John Lyly*, pp. 52–53).

17. *In* [*voluptate*] *spernenda et repudianda virtus vel maxime cernitur* (*De legibus*, I, 52).

18. Saker, *Narbonus. The Laberynth of Libertie* (1580) and Gosson, *The Ephemerides of Phialo* (1579). Other books referred to in the next several paragraphs are Gosson, *The Schoole of Abuse* (1579), Barnabe Rich, *The Straunge and Wonderfull Adventures of Don Simonides* (1581) and *The Second Tome of the Travailes and Adventures of Don Simonides* (1584), and Brian Melbancke, *Philotimus. The Warre betwixt Nature and Fortune* (1583).

19. OED, "prig." The quotation from *Count Fathom* (1784) fits *Euphues* rather well: "The templar is, generally speaking, a prig; so is the abbé: both are distinguished by an air of petulance and self-conceit, which holds a middle rank betwixt the insolence of a first-rate buck, and the learned pride of a supercilious pedant."

20. *School of Abuse* (1841; rpt. New York, 1970), p. 7.

21. William Ringler, *Stephen Gosson*, pp. 25–28.

22. *School of Abuse*, p. 4.

23. According to Spenser. See Ringler, *Gosson*, p. 37.

24. *Ibid.*, p. 49.
25. Davis, p. 131; Feuillerat, *John Lyly*, pp. 83–84.
26. Hunter, *Lyly*, p. 70.
27. See, for example, Horace's *Satire II, iii*, Terence's *Adelphi*, or Giovammaria Cecchi's *Figliuol Prodigo*. Another analogue to Lyly's opposition of avarice and prodigality is Ravisius Textor's *De Filio Prodigo* (*Dialogi*, 1530). Textor identifies the source of the first part of his dialogue, the satire on avarice, as Horace's *Epistle I, v.* "The second part," he writes, "is drawn from the well known story of the prodigal child." (*Secundum tractum est ex historia notissima de puero prodigo.*).
28. There was some backsliding on Rich's part, but he tried to cover it up. On the title page of his *Brusanus* (1592), he claimed that it was written "seven or eight years sithence," which would have put it back with the second tome of *Don Simonides* (1584). For evidence that he was lying and that the book was written shortly before it was published, see my "Lyly, Greene, Sidney, and Barnaby Rich's *Brusanus*," *HLQ*, 36 (1972/73), 105–118.
29. *Works*, ed. Bond, I. 26. Something of the same vestigal humanistic restraint can be seen in Lyly's comedies where the central characters—Alexander, Sappho, Cynthia, or Sophronia—end by refusing love.

5: GREENE

1. *Foure Letters and Certeine Sonnets, Especially Touching Robert Greene*, ed. G. B. Harrison (1922–1926; rpt. New York, 1966), pp. 20–21.
2. *The Life and Complete Works of Robert Greene*, ed. Alexander B. Grosart, 15 vols. (1881—1883; rpt. New York, 1964), XII, 155–156. Subsequent references to this edition will appear in the text.
3. Quoted by John Clark Jordan, *Robert Greene* (1915; rpt. New York, 1965), pp. 2–3.
4. *New York Review of Books*, 10 (23 May 1968), 22.
5. Jaroslav Hornát, "*Mamillia*: Robert Greene's Controversy with *Euphues*," *Philologica Pragensia*, 5 (1962), 210–218.
6. Cf. *Euphues*: "They say to abstain from pleasure is the chiefest piety" (Ed. Croll and Clemons, p. 180). See also p. 65, above.
7. For Greene's use of Greek romance see Samuel L. Wolff, *Greek Romances in Elizabethan Fiction* (New York, 1912), pp. 367–458. René Pruvost discusses each of Greene's fictions in terms of its probable sources and closest analogues in his *Robert Greene et ses romans* (Paris, 1938).
8. See my "Lyly, Greene, Sidney, and Barnaby Rich's *Brusanus*," *HLQ*, 36 (1972/73), 110 n. 9.
9. Though 1588 is the date of the earliest surviving edition of *Pandosto*, the book may have been written and published as much as four years earlier. An inventory of Roger Ward's Shrewsbury print shop, made in December 1584 or January 1585, includes among its entries "i9 Triumphe of time." There is good reason for identifying this as *Pandosto: The Triumph of Time*. The *Short-Title Catalogue* lists no

other "Triumph of Time," and we do know that Ward had dealings with Greene. Included in his stock were "i Antomy [sic] of fortune" and "7 mirror of modestie"—i.e., one copy of Greene's *Arbasto: The Anatomy of Fortune* and seven copies of his *Mirror of Modesty*, both published in 1584, the *Mirror* by Ward himself. I am kept, however, from adopting this earlier date by the fact that *Pandosto* shares a number of passages with Greene's *Euphues his Censure to Philautus* (1587), and the debt seems to be on *Pandosto*'s side. I suspect that only a careful reconsideration of the whole Greene canon, with particular attention given to self-plagiarism and plagiarism from other authors, will allow us to reconcile these contradictory bits of evidence. Until such a reconsideration has been completed, I think it prudent to date *Pandosto* 1588. For the Ward inventory, see Alexander Rodger, "Roger Ward's Shrewsbury Stock: an Inventory of 1585," *The Library*, 5th Ser., 13 (1958), 247–268.

10. Walter Davis discusses the passage from *Ciceronis Amor* relating it to other pastoral romances (*Idea and Act*, pp. 76–78). Davis (pp. 78–79) seems, however, to underestimate the pastoral element of *Pandosto*.

11. *Schoolmaster*, ed. Ryan, p. 69.

12. *Rich's Farewell to Military Profession*, ed. Thomas Mabry Cranfill (Austin, 1959), p. 204. Pettie (*Petite Palace*, ed. Hartman, p. 6) and Sidney (*Prose Works*, ed. Feuillerat, I, 4) also employ the self-depreciatory comparison of fiction and fashion. Another way of disarming critics common to Pettie, Lyly, Greene, and Sidney is to address one's work to gentle*women* readers—a simple way of announcing that one is dealing in trifles. A third possible line of defense which seems not to have occurred to Greene or to the translators of the novelle is to claim that the story conceals a moral allegory. This will be Harington's main argument in defending the *Orlando Furioso* (1591).

13. *The Works of Thomas Nashe*, ed. R. B. McKerrow, 5 vols. (1904; rev. and rpt. Oxford, 1958), I, 10.

14. Baker, *The Image of Man* (1947; rpt. New York, 1961), p. 248.

15. Pruvost (p. 323) suggests that Greene may have seen Nashe's satire in MS. This is plausible, but not necessary for my argument. Greene may already have been worrying about his reputation before Nashe further endangered it.

16. On the date of Greene's *Vision* see Jordan (p. 172) and Pruvost (p. 371).

17. Cf. Nashe (I, 27) where he approves stories that "include many profitable moral precepts, describing the outrage of unbridled youth, having the reins in their own hands, the fruits of idleness, the offspring of lust, and how available good educations are unto virtue."

18. Samuel L. Wolff, "Robert Greene and the Italian Renaissance," *Englische Studien*, 37 (1907), 346 n. 1.

19. This despite Greene's known distaste for the English Puritans. For a discussion of his part in the Marprelate Controversy see E. H. Miller, "The Relationship of Robert Greene and Thomas Nashe (1588–1592)," *PQ*, 33 (1954), 353–367.

20. *Institution de la Religion Chrétienne,* II, iv, 1. Calvin attributes the image to Augustine.

21. Recent suggestions that Chettle rather than Greene wrote the *Groatsworth of Wit,* even if true, do not seriously trouble my argument. Chettle would only have been giving further expression to an identification that Greene had established in a number of earlier works, works of unquestioned authorship, between himself and his prodigal protagonists. For a summary of the relevant bibliography, see *Shakespeare Newsletter,* 26 (1974), 47.

6: LODGE

1. *The Complete Works of Thomas Lodge,* ed. E.W. Gosse, 4 vols.(1883; rpt. New York, 1963), II, 55. Subsequent references to this edition will appear in the text. It should be noted that each work is separately paginated.

2. Quoted by Alice Walker, "The Reading of an Elizabethan," *RES,* 8 (1932), 266–267. It is on Walker's authority that I attribute the sentence from *Catharos* to the influence of Benedicti. I have been unable to check *La Somme des Pechez* myself.

3. Walker (p. 266) was the first to recognize Philoplutos as Burghley. She also suggested, with considerably more assurance, that Cosmosophos was Walsingham. I am less convinced than she of the accuracy of the latter identification, and more sure of the former. In addition to the evidence she cites, one might note that Philoplutos appears riding a mule, a pose Burghley adopted in a portrait frequently reproduced in the sixteenth century, and that he calls himself *pater patriae,* a sobriquet often applied to Burghley.

4. *Thomas Lodge and Other Elizabethans* (Cambridge, 1933), p. 160.

5. See, for example, Frank Cioffi, "Intention and Interpretation in Criticism," *Proceedings of the Aristotelian Society,* 64 (1963/64), 85–106, Quentin Skinner, "Meaning and Understanding in the History of Ideas," *History and Theory,* 8 (1969), 3–53, Michael H. Black, "Why It Is So, and Not Otherwise," *NLH,* 6 (1974/75), 477–489, and John R. Searle, *Speech Acts* (Cambridge, 1969) and "The Logical Status of Fiction," *NLH,* 6 (1974/75), 319–332.

6. *Playes Confuted in Five Actions,* ed. W. C. Hazlitt in *The English Drama and Stage* (1832; rpt. New York, 1969), p. 160.

7. Sisson, p. 102.

8. Edward Andrews Tenney, *Thomas Lodge* (1935; rpt. New York, 1969), p. 86. Cf. Sisson (p. 156), "The *Alarm . . .* may have been partly meant to soften the old man's heart towards his ill-used second son."

9. Sisson, p. 156–157.

10. "Masking in Arden: The Histrionics of Lodge's *Rosalynde,*" *SEL,* 5 (1965), 163. Davis's interpretation of *Rosalind* reappears in an altered form in his *Idea and Act in Elizabethan Fiction,* pp. 83–93.

11. Euphues' testament was omitted from the first edition of *Rosa-*

lind, apparently by mistake since neither the subtitle nor the epilogue make sense without it.

12. The phrase "second self" comes from W. B. Yeats by way of Davis, "Masking," p. 163.

13. Tenney, pp. 111–112. Tenney supplies a fuller list of sources than I have here reproduced.

14. *Ibid.,* pp. 160–162.

15. *Schoolmaster,* ed. Ryan, p. 68.

16. For Nashe see Tenney, p. 130–131; for Greene see Philip Drew, "Was Greene's 'Young Juvenal' Nashe or Lodge?" *SEL,* 7 (1967), 55–56; for T. B. see Walker, pp. 266–267. Drew is not certain whether Greene was addressing Lodge or Nashe, but suggests "that the balance of evidence is in Lodge's favor." T. B.'s reaction to *Catharos,* which Drew fails to mention, tips the balance even further.

7: SIDNEY

1. *Trewnesse of the Christian Religion* (1587), Sig. * 3ᵛ. (UMEES, Reel 440.)

2. *Works,* ed. McKerrow, I, 159.

3. In a technical sense Sidney might be counted a prodigal. He continually spent more than he had. But neither his contemporaries nor his conscience held that against him. Lavish expenditure was expected in one of his great station. One recent critic has, however, taken Sidney to task for his financial improvidence. See R. A. Lanham, "Sidney: The Ornament of his Age," *Southern Review,* 2 (1967), 329–331.

4. "An Elegie, or friends passion, for his Astrophill," *The Phoenix Nest (1593),* ed. Hyder Edward Rollins (Cambridge, Mass., 1931), p. 13.

5. George Gregory Smith, *Elizabethan Critical Essays,* 2 vols. (Oxford, 1904), II, 263.

6. *A Poetical Rhapsody,* ed. H. E. Rollins, 2 vols. (Cambridge, Mass., 1931), I, 5.

7. Sir Fulke Greville, *Life of Sir Philip Sidney,* ed. Nowell Smith (Oxford, 1907), pp. 11–18; Sir John Harington, *Orlando Furioso* (1591), Sig. iiᵛ–viiiᵛ (Harington bases the "Apologie of Poetrie" which he prefixes to his *OF* on Sidney's and quotes AS 18 in defense of love in the notes to *OF* XVI); Harvey in Smith, II, 263–264; Edwin Greenlaw, "Sidney's *Arcadia* as an Example of Elizabethan Allegory," *Kittredge Anniversary Papers* (Boston, 1913), pp. 327–337; Kenneth Myrick, *Sir Philip Sidney as a Literary Craftsman* (Cambridge, Mass., 1935); Neil L. Rudenstine, *Sidney's Poetic Development* (Cambridge, Mass., 1967); Walter R. Davis, *Idea and Act in Elizabethan Fiction,* pp. 28–69; see also Davis's earlier *Map of Arcadia* (New Haven, 1965); Jon S. Lawry, *Sidney's Two Arcadias: Pattern and Proceeding* (Ithaca, N.Y., 1972).

8. Harvey in Smith, II, 263; Greville, p. 16; *Phoenix Nest*, p. 14.

9. *Apology for Poetry*, ed. Geoffrey Shepherd (Edinburgh, 1965), p. 101. Subsequent references to the *Apology* will be to this edition and will appear in the text.

10. Greville, p. 18.

11. The phrase "impure persuasion" is from Kenneth Burke by way of a recent article by R. A. Lanham, "*Astrophil and Stella*: Pure and Impure Persuasion," *ELR*, 2 (1972), 100–115. Russell Fraser has also been at pains to point out the impurity of Sidney's aesthetic in "Sidney the Humanist," *South Atlantic Quarterly*, 46 (1967), 87–91.

12. Greville, pp. 16–17.

13. *The Prose Works of Sir Philip Sidney*, ed. Albert Feuillerat (1912–1926; rpt. Cambridge, 1962), I, 113 and 403. Subsequent references to Feuillerat's *Sidney* will appear in the text.

14. See Catherine Barnes's careful analysis of the various ways in which Sidney qualifies his defense of poetry. "The Hidden Persuader: The Complex Speaking Voice of Sidney's *Defence of Poetry*," *PMLA*, 86 (1971), 422–427.

15. The allegorical association of self-love with foolish prodigality provides another example of the relation between humanistic moral philosophy and prodigal son literature. In Erasmus' *Encomium* Philautia accompanies Folly; in both *Acolastus* and *The Anatomy of Wit* the friend of the prodigal is called Philautus; and in *The Glass of Government* one of the two prodigals himself bears that name.

16. Lanham, "*Astrophil and Stella*," p. 104.

17. Katherine Duncan-Jones and Jan van Dorsten, *Miscellaneous Prose of Sir Philip Sidney* (Oxford, 1973), p. 134.

18. *The Countess of Pembroke's Arcadia (The Old Arcadia)*, ed. Jean Robertson (Oxford, 1973), p. 430 (note to p. 71). Subsequent references to the Old *Arcadia* will be to this edition and will appear in the text. I follow, however, the recommendation of Franklin B. Williams, Jr., in writing "Evarchus" rather than "Euarchus." See William's review of Robertson, *Renaissance Quarterly*, 27 (1974), 240–242.

19. Harvey in Smith, II, 263.

20. See Robertson, p. 431 (note to p. 73, 11. 12–14).

21. Henry Thomas, "Diana de Monte Mayor Done out of Spanish by Thomas Wilson (1596)," *Revue Hispanique*, 50 (1920), 372.

22. Quoted by Thomas McFarland, *Shakespeare's Pastoral Comedy* (Chapel Hill, N.C., 1972), pp. 68–69.

23. The most thorough examination of these matters is E. G. Fogel's "The Personal References in the Fiction and Poetry of Sir Philip Sidney" (Ph.D. diss., Ohio State University, 1958).

24. "Sidney's Original *Arcadia*," *The London Mercury*, 15 (1927), 514.

25. *Sidney's Poetic Development*, p. 16.

26. The various clues to the moral truancy of Pyrocles and Musidorus have been exhaustively examined by recent critics. On the bear, the lion, and the Phagonian rebels, see Elizabeth Dipple, "Harmony and Pastoral in the *Old Arcadia*," *ELH*, 35 (1968), 309–328, and Franco Marenco, "Double Plot in Sidney's Old *Arcadia*," *MLR*, 64 (1969),

248–263. On the transvestism, see Mark Rose, "Sidney's Womanish Man," *RES*, n.s. 15 (1964), 353–363. On the dark cave, see Walter R. Davis, "Acteon in Arcadia," *SEL*, 2 (1962), 95–110. On the schemes of desire, see Franco Marenco, *L'Arcadia Puritana* (Bari, 1968).

27. *"Astrophil and Stella,"* p. 107.

28. *The Poems of Sir Philip Sidney*, ed. William A. Ringler, Jr. (Oxford, 1962). All references to *Astrophel and Stella* are to his edition. I differ from Ringler, however, in spelling "Astrophel" with an "e" rather than an "i". He has logic on his side; I have euphony. There is early MS support for both spellings (Ringler, p. 458).

29. Pears, *Correspondence*, pp. 6 and 25.

30. I am not here following Ringler's punctuation. He gives "But ah" to Desire. I think it belongs to Astrophel.

31. For a suggestive examination of the figure of Urania in the New *Arcadia* see K. D. Duncan-Jones, "Sidney's Urania," *RES*, n.s. 17 (1966), 123–132.

32. See Ringler (pp. 375–378) and W. L. Godshalk ("Sidney's Revision of the *Arcadia*, Books III-V," *PQ*, 43 [1964], 171–184) both of whom argue for Sidney's responsibility. However, Sidney's retention in the Oracle of the lines "Thy younger shall with Nature's bliss embrace/An uncouth love, which Nature hateth most" (Feuillerat, I, 327) puts the reformation of Pyrocles—by far the most important change—in doubt.

33. Myrick, p. 237. See also Fogel's chapter on "Personal Touches in the Two *Arcadias*."

34. See above, pp. 11. .

35. *Nobilis, or a View of the Life and Death of a Sidney*, trans. and ed. Virgil B. Heltzel and Hoyt H. Hudson (San Marino, Calif., 1940), p. 74.

36. J. C. A. Rathmell, *The Psalms of Sir Philip Sidney and the Countess of Pembroke* (Garden City, N.Y., 1963), p. xxv.

37. *Miscellaneous Prose*, p. 169.

38. Robert Kimborough, *Sir Philip Sidney* (New York, 1971), p. 15.

39. Du Bartas's *Semaine* was first published in 1578 and Mornay's *Vérité* in 1581. These dates, at least, rule out the period prior to the writing of the Old *Arcadia*. The only other evidence proves nothing about the dates of Sidney's translations. We know that he had read *La Semaine* by 1582, when he used it in *Astrophel and Stella* (Ringler, p. 339), and the *Vérité* by 1583, when it was used for the New *Arcadia* (D. P. Walker, "Ways of Dealing with Atheists: A Background to Pamela's Refutation of Cecropia," *Bibliothèque d'humanisme et renaissance*, 17 [1953], 252-277). As for the Psalms, according to Ringler (p. 500), "the evidence available suggests that Sidney began work late in his career, perhaps not long before his departure for the Netherlands in 1585."

40. Myrick, p. 21.

41. Mentioned by J. A. van Dorsten, "Sidney and Languet," *HLQ*, 29 (1965/66), 215–216.

42. From Sidney's letter to Denny in Osborne, *Young Philip Sidney*, p. 537.

Index